brilliant

cognitive behavioural therapy

second edition

How to use CBT to improve your mind and your life

Dr Stephen Briers

PEARSON

Harlow, England • London • New York • Boston • San Francisco • Toronto • Sydney • Auckland • Singapore • Hong Kong
Tokyo • Seoul • Taipei • New Delhi • Cape Town • São Paulo • Mexico City • Madrid • Amsterdam • Munich • Paris • Milan

PEARSON EDUCATION LIMITED

Edinburgh Gate
Harlow CM20 2JE
Tel: +44 (0)1279 623623
Fax: +44 (0)1279 431059
Website: www.pearson.com/uk

First published 2009 (print)
Second edition published 2012 (print and electronic)

Pearson Education is not responsible for the content of third-party internet sites.

ISBN: 978-0-273-77773-1 (print)
ISBN: 978-0-273-77850-9 (PDF)
ISBN: 978-0-273-77849-3 (ePub)

British Library Cataloguing-in-Publication Data
A catalogue record for the print edition is available from the British Library

Library of Congress Cataloging-in-Publication Data
A catalog record for the print edition is available from the Library of Congress

10 9 8 7 6 5 4 3 2 1
16 15 14 13 12

Cartoons by Bill Piggins except where noted
Print edition typeset in 10/14pt Plantin Std by 30
Print edition printed in Great Britain by Henry Ling Ltd, at the Dorset Press, Dorchester, DT1 1HD

NOTE THAT ANY PAGE CROSS REFERENCES REFER TO THE PRINT EDITION

Contents

About the author

Before training as a clinical psychologist, Dr Stephen Briers studied at Cambridge University where he was later employed in child development research at the Winnicott Unit.

Today Stephen works clinically with both children and adults. His various television appearances include four series of the popular BBC parenting programmes *Little Angels* and *Teen Angels* and *Make Me A Grown-Up* for Channel 4. He has formerly been a regular contributor to the *Brain and Behaviour* column in *The Times Educational Supplement* and is author of *Superpowers for Parents*.

He lives and works in Brighton with his wife and two teenage sons.

Author's acknowledgements

Many thanks to family and friends who have put up with me during the writing of this book. I am sure we will all reframe it as the best of times! Thanks also to the publishing team at Pearson for all their hard work. I also owe a great debt to the many clients who have provided the material on which many of the case examples in this book are based. Names and identifying details have, of course, been changed. Finally, I would like to dedicate this book to you, the reader, for taking the time to read it and having the courage to aim for a better future.

Publisher's acknowledgements

We are grateful to the following for permission to reproduce copyright material:

Cartoon on p.16 by Chris Madden; Alamy Images: p.33, imagestopshop / Alamy; p.37, INTERFOTO / Alamy; Savage Chickens cartoon 'Anger' on p.183 by Doug Savage, cartoon on p.218 from Cartoon Stock, www.cartoonstock.com; figure on p.274 from *Applied Cognitive and Behavioural Approaches to the Treatment of Addiction*, Mitcheson, L., Maslin, J. et al. © 2010. Reproduced with permission of John Wiley & Sons Ltd.

Every effort has been made by the publisher to obtain permission from the appropriate source to reproduce material which appears in this book. In some instances we may have been unable to trace the owners of copyright material and would appreciate any information that would enable us to do so.

CHAPTER 1

So what's so brilliant about CBT?

When you think about the word 'therapy', what comes to mind? A few years ago the term was commonly associated with couches and tears, brooding silences and the painstaking excavation of childhood fantasies and buried memories. This was due to the influence of the school of psychoanalysis founded by Sigmund Freud in the nineteenth century, one which came to dominate popular conceptions of therapy for most of the twentieth century.

However, in recent decades a revolution has taken place. A very different model of treatment has emerged that has not only challenged many of these preconceptions, but has now successfully established itself as the most widely practised form of talking cure in the world. This model – which is actually a synthesis of several different theoretical traditions – is known as Cognitive Behavioural Therapy or CBT for short.

When the first edition of this book was published, CBT's star was already in the ascendant. Its meteoric rise has continued and, if anything, even been accelerating ever since. Three years on, CBT looks as if it has not only changed the face of mental healthcare for ever, but its principles are routinely being applied in schools, businesses and a variety of other non-clinical settings. CBT is definitely no longer the new kid on the block. It's everywhere and, if you have picked up this book, you will almost certainly have heard of it. When 'therapy' is mentioned these days, people are just as likely to call to mind aspects of

CBT as they are to reach for the stereotypes and clichés of Freudian psychoanalysis.

In the UK, the profile of CBT has been raised significantly by government initiatives aimed at ensuring that more and more of us can have access to CBT on the National Health Service. At the end of the six-year rollout of the IAPT (Improving Access to Psychological Therapies) programme an additional 6000 new CBT therapists will have been trained. The goal is to make sure that by 2015 every adult that requires it should have access to psychological therapies to treat anxiety disorder or depression. However, the second phase of IAPT is also seeking to make CBT more available to children and young people, those suffering from long-term physical conditions, unexplained medical symptoms and even people with severe mental illnesses. CBT is increasingly regarded as the 'treatment of choice' for an ever-expanding menu of mental health problems by the National Institute of Clinical Excellence (NICE). Pioneering studies have recently been exploring the role of CBT in alleviating symptoms of epilepsy, heart disease, back pain, breast cancer and even menopausal hot flushes. It seems that scarcely a week passes without news of CBT's successful application to yet another new problem or client group.

Innovative new ways of delivering CBT are also being developed all the time. In January 2012 an article in The Lancet reported on a small-scale study providing CBT interventions through videoconferencing and mobile phones. Even more intriguingly, a team from the University of Auckland has recently created a computer-based fantasy, role-playing game called SPARX designed to help young people learn skills to combat the symptoms of depression. If you fancy, you can take a look at the SPARX trailer for yourself on YouTube. Several websites now offer computerised CBT packages online and there are some excellent smartphone applications available to help you put CBT techniques into practice. If you are interested, you can find an overview of some of these in Appendix 1 at the end of this book.

This book aims to introduce you to both the theory and practice of CBT so you can start applying this powerful tool in your own life. The following pages will help you to:

- appreciate some of the distinctive features of the cognitive behavioural approach
- familiarise yourself with CBT's basic principles, methods and models
- learn how to structure your own problems within the framework that CBT offers
- spot unhelpful patterns of thought and behaviour that may be contributing to your difficulties
- create practical, step-by-step strategies for tackling your problems using established cognitive behavioural techniques.

As you progress there will be exercises to help you develop your understanding of CBT techniques and the main points will be illustrated using real-life examples. I have also included some trouble-shooting tips to help you achieve the results you want.

The origins of CBT: giving Freud the slip

'Turning on the intercom...': this is how Aaron Temkin Beck described the breakthrough responsible for the evolution of CBT. In the 1960s Beck was an established (if rather frustrated) psychiatrist attempting to treat his patients using Freudian psychoanalysis. While Freud's methods emphasised the importance of unpacking repressed conflicts from the past, Beck became convinced that for many of his patients the crux of their problems lay more in what they were telling themselves in the present.

He took up this line of inquiry when one of his patients admitted a number of anxious thoughts about how the consultation with Beck was going. The patient noticed several thoughts of the following kind running through his head:

- *'I am a bad patient.'*
- *'Dr Beck will be disappointed in me.'*
- *'I am just wasting his time... He will probably want to stop seeing me...'*

Beck became convinced that, whatever their original source, it was this anxiety-laden commentary that was driving his patient's unpleasant emotions in the here and now. For Beck 'turning on the intercom' meant giving patients and therapists access to their internal monologue – the stream of characteristic fleeting thoughts that raced through their heads whenever they felt depressed, anxious or unsure of themselves.

It occurred to Beck that if his patients' emotional problems were being caused by their characteristic thinking style, then training them to adopt alternative 'healthier' habits of thought might provide the key to relieving their symptoms.

Beck developed these promising insights and started putting them to the test in his clinical practice. In 1979 he published *Cognitive Therapy of Depression*, a landmark text that not only described the hallmarks of a depressive thinking style but offered a new approach for correcting them. Since that time CBT has never looked back.

 exercise   Pause for thought

Think of a time in your life when you felt particularly unhappy, fearful or stressed. Can you recall the sorts of thoughts that went through your head when you were in that state? How did you see yourself? Other people? The future?

Next time you are in a situation in which upsetting emotions wash over you, try to become aware of changes in your thinking by tuning into your thoughts and impressions. Do they have a distinctive character or quality at odds with the way you see things when feeling calmer or more upbeat?

Beck's basic principles have been adapted and customised to create treatment packages for a huge range of conditions. Originally most closely associated with the treatment of depression and anxiety, CBT protocols now exist to help cancer patients stop smoking, to assist unemployed people get back into the workforce and to support those who suffer with more intractable mental health issues like personality disorders and psychosis. Aspects of traditional CBT are also being combined with elements of other therapeutic approaches and traditions to create an innovative raft of new therapies including Acceptance and Commitment Therapy (ACT), Mindfulness-based CBT and Cognitive Analytic Therapy (CAT). The table below gives you a very brief introduction to how CBT is continuing to evolve and play a part in shaping a new generation of 'hybrid' therapies.

A brilliant (but brief) guide to some common therapies and their relationship to CBT

Name of therapy	Description	Relation to CBT
Psychoanalytic/ Psychodynamic therapy	Psychoanalysis aims to develop self-awareness and bring unconscious conflicts to the surface. Often associated with the influence of childhood experience and Freud's theories of sexuality.	CBT usually focuses more on how problems manifest and are maintained in the present rather than concentrating on early childhood experiences. Although they seem very different both psychoanalysis and CBT share an interest in the sense that we make of our experience. In psychoanalysis the relationship with the therapist is a context in which the client plays out and projects important unresolved feelings. In CBT the role of the therapist is more one of mentor and guide.

Name of therapy	Description	Relation to CBT
Mindfulness-based therapy	Rooted in eastern meditation traditions that emphasise the importance of being present in the moment. Mindfulness trains people to de-centre themselves and observe their emotions and thoughts in a non-judgemental way. By accepting that they are temporary, negative thoughts and feelings are allowed to pass freely in and out of consciousness.	At first glance, Mindfulness appears to be at odds with CBT, which generally focuses on modifying upsetting thoughts rather than teaching people to tolerate them. However, Segal, Williams and Teasdale have pioneered a version of CBT that integrates elements of the mindfulness approach and has proved very effective in preventing relapse in depression.
Acceptance and Commitment Therapy (ACT)	Like Mindfulness, ACT encourages people to neutralise distressing thoughts and feelings by just 'noticing' them and creating a sense of an observing self that stands back from one's experience.	ACT places more emphasis than CBT on discovering and bringing one's actions into alignment with personal values.
Dialectical Behaviour Therapy (DBT)	Developed as a treatment for borderline personality disorder, DBT focuses on helping sufferers evaluate the usefulness of their thoughts, manage distressing emotions and develop more appropriate social skills to get their needs met.	Many of the techniques used in DBT are based on a combination of cognitive behavioural techniques and mindfulness principles. DBT emphasises the role of the therapist in both validating the client's feelings and simultaneously challenging behaviours and attitudes that can cause problems for them.

Name of therapy	Description	Relation to CBT
Person-centred counselling	Derived from the work of humanistic psychologist Carl Rogers who believed that provided with unconditional regard and a facilitating, supportive relationship, most people will spontaneously gravitate towards healthier and more functional states of mind.	Person-centred counselling is explicitly non-directive. The therapist encourages a client to explore issues and asks pertinent open questions but does not lead the client or attempt to teach specific skills to modulate thoughts, emotions or behaviours as in CBT.
Compassion Focused Therapy (CFT)	A form of CBT developed by Paul Gilbert that encourages people to accept their feelings and develop compassion-based cognitions that activate the self-soothing systems of the brain.	Like CBT, CFT emphasises the content of negative thoughts but tends to target those that give rise to feelings of shame and self-criticism. Unlike most forms of CBT, CFT aims to induce specific emotional and mental states using imagery and self-affirmations, rather than rationalising unwanted thoughts using logic and trying to generate 'balanced' alternatives.

Name of therapy	Description	Relation to CBT
Brief solution-focused therapy	A set of techniques created by Steve de Shazer and Insoo Kim Berg, solution-focused therapy aims to help people find clues to solving problems by analysing existing situations in which their problems have less influence on them, or imagining scenarios in which the problem has already been resolved. The idea is that if people can behave 'as if' the problem has gone then they will adopt patterns of thought and action that will help alleviate it.	Like CBT, solution-focused interventions stress the contribution of an individual's difficulties as thoughts, feelings and behaviours in perpetuating their difficulties. Even more than CBT, solution-focused therapy is interested exclusively in how the problem manifests itself in the present. Its past antecedents are considered largely irrelevant.
Cognitive Analytic Therapy (CAT)	CAT is a treatment that usually helps people understand and compensate for the way their early relationships have shaped their behaviour in the present. Symptoms are usually as side effects of unhelpful coping styles.	As the name suggests CAT is a hybrid of cognitive approaches and psychoanalytic theory. To the first it owes an emphasis on tackling dysfunctional thought patterns and assumptions; to the latter an emphasis on psychological defence mechanisms and the way we internalise mental models of early relationships with key carers. Like CBT, CAT is usually time-limited. One of its hallmarks is the summary letters exchanged between therapist and client.

Name of therapy	Description	Relation to CBT
Neuro-Linguistic Programming (NLP)	NLP is not really a cohesive therapy but a ragbag of different techniques without a particularly clear theoretical basis. It claims to unlock individual potential by teaching individuals to model the behaviours and thought processes of successful and high-functioning people.	Like CBT, NLP is interested in changing unhelpful thought patterns and breaking destructive cycles. As in CBT, proponents of NLP claim that the mind can be taught to learn new, more helpful patterns. However, where CBT and NLP part company is that NLP has proved very difficult to assess in clinical trials, so its evidence base is virtually non-existent. Although many claim that its teachings have genuinely helped them, NLP has been accused of being pseudo-science and is certainly not endorsed by NICE.

Why is CBT so popular?

Recently, CBT has attracted considerable attention. Its current popularity lies not only in its relevance to such a broad variety of emotional issues, but also in its 'goodness of fit' with the priorities and values of our times.

It is accessible

Sometimes dubbed the 'psychology of common sense' CBT is much more readily understood than the complex and sometimes counterintuitive theories of Freud and Jung. By mapping out the way in which our thoughts, feelings and actions all affect each other, with a little practice it becomes relatively straightforward to identify targets and strategies for dealing with whatever issues you may be facing.

It is skills-based

CBT is rooted in an educational approach. Therapy is not about being 'fixed' by an expert but rather learning the skills you need to solve your own problems and look after your own mental health. One criticism levelled at conventional therapy is that it can make clients emotionally dependent upon their therapist. In CBT such dependence is actively discouraged: the therapist is someone who comes alongside to facilitate and equip, and many people find this way of working less threatening. However, you always need to find the approach that is right for you.

> you always need to find the approach that is right for you

It has a proven track record

CBT is all about evidence, so it is no surprise that from the outset Beck and his followers were fairly rigorous about measuring its effectiveness. CBT is probably better researched than most other forms of therapy and always seeks to define patients' gains in concrete, observable terms. This can be quite hard to do within the psychoanalytic tradition. In this form of treatment progress is so wrapped up in individual experience that it can prove hard to measure in scientific terms. In making its current recommendations for which psychological treatments are most appropriate for various common mental health conditions, NICE has based its 2011 guidelines on a comprehensive review of the available research literature, much of which has been summarised by Anthony Roth and Peter Fonagy in the latest edition of their book *What Works for Whom?*

Conditions for which NICE recommends CBT as a treatment of choice

Major depressive disorder	☑
Bipolar disorder	☑
Schizophrenia	☑
Generalised anxiety disorder	☑
Panic disorder	☑
Obsessive compulsive disorder	☑
Post traumatic stress disorder	☑
Bulimia	☑
Anorexia nervosa	☑
Alcoholism	☑
Conduct disorder in older children	☑

The fact that CBT can defend its claims using research evidence has made it all the more appealing to the modern NHS. However, it is worth remembering that even the most painstaking research has its limitations. At the end of the day even highly impressive research trial results are no guarantee that a treatment will work for a particular individual.

It can deliver rapid results

One of the major selling points of CBT is that the basic principles can be mastered relatively quickly. This means that whereas traditional psychotherapy can involve several years of weekly sessions, most courses of CBT are time-limited, aiming to equip people with the skills they need in just a few months. In May 2012 there was a heartening report of how only 15 sessions of CBT had reduced the trauma symptoms of child victims of war-torn central Africa by more than 50%. Since the results of such brief interventions compare favourably with other more time-intensive therapies, one can understand why for healthcare services juggling limited budgets the CBT model of treatment fits the bill – quite literally. For example, the NICE guidelines cite possible net savings of £1000 per person for every person treated for schizophrenia using CBT. The fact that research often suggests a relatively brief CBT intervention can also be a clinically effective one leaves healthcare providers quite naturally feeling they are looking at a win–win situation. This is why the British government is ploughing millions into developing CBT-based services.

Will it work for me?

One of the great strengths of CBT is that its principles and techniques potentially have such widespread applications. At its heart is a model of the mind that focuses on how we make sense of our experience and how that process can backfire and cause problems for us.

In fact, although CBT is associated with the treatment of diag-nosable conditions, it is increasingly being used to improve performance in situations that have little to do with mental health. After all, most of us will have something to gain from a system which helps us to develop habits of rationality and healthy mindedness, and strengthens the ability to handle the emotional challenges life throws at us.

Below is a checklist of questions to help you make an informed choice about whether CBT will work for you. Simply circle the number that most applies to you.

Question 1: *How self-disciplined are you?*

Not at all   Very much so

You are embarking on a mission to change mental habits that have been reinforced over a very long period, quite possibly a lifetime. That's going to require some self-discipline: anyone who has attempted to break a habit of any kind, from smoking to weight gain, already knows how hard this can be.

To benefit from CBT you will have to keep conscientious records of your thoughts, feelings and behaviour, often at the very times you feel least inclined to do so because you feel angry, stressed or fed up. However, make no mistake: CBT is not a quick fix or magic wand. It will only work if you persevere. Busy schedules and frantic lifestyles can make it hard to get the most out of the techniques so be prepared to make some room in your life to do your homework if you want to get the most out of CBT.

> make no mistake: CBT is not a quick fix or magic wand

Question 2: *How open-minded are you?*

Not at all   Very much so

The essence of CBT is learning to challenge preconceptions about ourselves, other people and the world at large. You must be ready to put even taken-for-granted or cherished convictions in the dock and examine them in the light of the hard evidence.

This can be exciting but also unsettling. We are often strongly invested in our assumptions about things – even if those assumptions aren't helping us. The beliefs that are the most rigid are often the ones that hold us back, and if you are the kind of person who has to win every argument, sees things in black and white, or always has to have the last word, then CBT may be quite challenging for you. Having said that, you may also have the most to gain.

'IT'S A WONDERFUL IDEA, BUT CAN'T WE HAVE SOMETHING A BIT MORE POETIC – SUCH AS THE EARTH BALANCED ON THE BACK OF A CROCODILE FLOATING IN A SEA OF MAMMOTH'S MILK?'

Question 3: *Are you prepared to take a long, hard look at yourself?*

Not at all   Very much so

Although traditional psychotherapy often gets lumbered with associations of introspection and 'navel-gazing', cognitive behavioural methods require no less self-scrutiny. You will be examining your thought patterns and behaviour in fine detail and observing yourself intently in different settings.

You also have to be prepared for the fact that you may not like everything you discover about yourself. None of us really relish criticism, however constructive and helpful, and during the CBT process you may well be encouraged to open yourself up to candid feedback from other people.

Question 4: *Are you prepared to step out of your comfort zone?*

Not at all   Very much so

CBT does not just require you to take a 'warts and all' look at yourself and your behaviour. Often, its methods may require you to engage in experiments designed literally to push you to your limits. Challenging entrenched assumptions is best achieved by testing them out.

Say you hold a conviction that everyone will stare at you if you get anxious and start sweating: would you be prepared to deliberately soak your shirt with water and head out for the local shopping centre to see what happens? This is precisely the sort of task that you may end up setting yourself.

As this example implies, the situations that make us the most anxious are precisely the ones we try to avoid. CBT will ask you to do things that will feel counterintuitive, scary and just plain wrong in the interests of helping you break cycles of fear and misery that keep you trapped. It's message to you may well be that you need to confront the very things you have been avoiding and see that the results are not as bad as you supposed. You need to ask yourself: are you really prepared for that? CBT is not for the faint-hearted.

Question 5: *How much do you like solving problems?*

Not at all   Very much so

Some people love puzzles. Other people can't be bothered with them. If you are intending to use the techniques in this book without the help of a trained therapist who would do some of the work for you, then you will need to work in a systematic, analytical fashion as you gradually work out what is going on and spot patterns in your life that need to be changed. Setting goals, trying things out, and finding a better way is at the heart of the CBT approach.

One advantage of CBT is that it does encourage you to isolate specific areas of difficulty and work on localised problems rather than dealing with the whole picture all at once. Breaking things down into manageable chunks and generating solutions to specific issues is very much the way that CBT aims to shift the bigger emotional mountains that can otherwise leave us feeling intimidated and overwhelmed.

brilliant example

'What's the problem? What *isn't* a problem? Since Paulo was born it feels like our whole world has been ripped apart.' This was the opening response of Anita, a young woman who came into therapy with a diagnosis of severe postnatal depression.

Anita went on to list a catalogue of difficulties she and her husband were facing: since the birth he had lost his job and was struggling to cope with Anita's low mood; there were issues as to whether Anita's elderly mother would come and live with them; they were disagreeing about how Paulo should be brought up... . Her therapist stopped her. 'I can see things feel really difficult for you at the moment,' he said, 'but if you could change just one thing right now what would it be?' 'I just want to feel some connection with my baby,' Anita replied sadly.

It was agreed that under the circumstances this was a long-term goal that might take some time to achieve, but together Anita and her psychologist brainstormed some practical steps that might bring Anita a little closer to this objective. Spending time trying to interact with Paulo was just making her feel self-conscious and even more of a failure, so a plan was made that every day Anita would strap her son into a sling that held him close to her body and they would go for a half-hour walk in the countryside together.

After a while, Anita discovered that as she and Paulo took their afternoon walk the combination of physical contact and a pocket of relatively stress-free time in each other's company began to kindle a stronger attachment between them. Anita spontaneously began chatting to Paulo as they walked, pointing out trees and birds to him. She was surprised by how instinctive this became. As her confidence in her relationship with her son increased, Anita felt less fazed by the other difficulties she was facing, and became more mentally and emotionally available to start tackling them in therapy.

Question 6: *How good are you at tuning in to your feelings?*

Not at all   Very much so

CBT requires us to become conscious of the thoughts and feelings that affect us negatively but these thought patterns are not always readily available. Some people manage difficult emotions and thoughts by blocking them out of awareness.

To work well CBT requires us to be able to separate out the different strands of our feelings because each element can point to quite different thoughts. For example, if I am conscious I am 'fed up' that may not help me tap into the same types of thoughts that enable me to recognise that my 'fed up-ness' is actually a combination of sadness (20%), anger (40%), frustration (25%) and loneliness (15%).

If you do find it hard to tune into your emotions then CBT can be an uphill struggle, although as you practise recording your moods and emotions you may be surprised by how much better you get. It is a bit like learning to familiarise yourself with a new language or appreciate a different type of music.

brilliant tip

Expand your emotional vocabulary

As you get better at describing your feelings you will automatically become more attuned to them. Try developing a more expansive vocabulary for your emotions that allows you to make more precise

▶

distinctions between your moods. Rather than just relying on everyday labels like 'happy' and 'sad' make the effort to pinpoint your feelings more precisely by learning some more of the 3000 plus words the English language provides to describe emotions.

Question 7: *How easy did you find it to rate yourself on these items?*

Not at all   Very much so

No, not a trick question. I have already mentioned that CBT loves to measure things, and you will regularly be asked to gauge the intensity and frequency of your thoughts and feelings. You won't have to be deadly accurate and again this is a skill you can learn as you go along. However, if you are one of those people (and I rank myself in their number) who finds personality quizzes difficult because 'sometimes I am like this and sometimes a bit like that' then CBT may prove quite testing for you at times. To paraphrase the nuns in *The Sound of Music*, when it comes to quantifying your thoughts and feelings, CBT can feel very much like trying 'to catch a cloud and pin it down'. But with practice you'll soon get the hang of it. However, it really can be helpful to develop this skill because at the point you recognise, for example, that your anxiety level has dropped from a 7 to a 3, you know you are getting somewhere!

> CBT can feel like trying 'to catch a cloud and pin it down'

How did you do?

If you found yourself scoring between 0 and 2 on more than four items I would suggest you either consider another form of therapy or at least try CBT with the support of a trained practitioner who can help you in the areas that may come less easily to you.

However, also recognise that where you score now on these scales is not necessarily indicative of where you will end up after practising some of the techniques described in this book. Low scores certainly do not rule CBT out of the equation. It simply means that there may be some aspects of the approach that may demand more from you. If you do find yourself struggling to apply the techniques you read about in the rest of this book, don't forget you can always consult the trouble-shooting guide on page 273.

It is always helpful to be aware of potential pitfalls and hazards from the outset and to make informed choices. Then you can prepare yourself and develop strategies to compensate – a very CBT way to approach matters.

exercise

I admit it: I always skip these kinds of tasks in books too. However, if you were seeing a psychologist for treatment you would probably be doing something similar to this exercise in the initial session. The reason is that people who reflect actively upon their motivations and their own learning process do tend to engage better, learn more deeply and stick with it when difficulties present themselves.

So, before you proceed any further, sit down somewhere quiet and attempt to answer the following questions:

▶

- What am I hoping to gain from learning more about CBT?

- What difficulties am I likely to face as I attempt to put the advice in this book into practice? (For example, consider when you will make time to practise techniques or whether there are aspects of your personality that might make it difficult for you to get to grips with the approach.)

- Is there anything I can do to help myself overcome any potential difficulties?

- What difference will CBT make to my life?

Now read on...

By now you are hopefully starting to have a sense of what CBT is all about. The level of commotion surrounding this relatively new therapy is extraordinary, but behind the hype there are sound, tried and tested psychological principles and insights that deliver results. It is not a quick fix, but the nature of CBT is such that most people should be able to enjoy significant benefits from the approach, even without the help of a professional therapist. If you think you might be one of those people, brilliant reader, then read on...

CHAPTER 2

First principles

I n this chapter you will be given an overview of the CBT model of the mind and introduced to the five key principles upon which it depends. To any reader eager to get stuck in, please don't be tempted to rush through the next few pages. Unless you grasp the underlying principles, and have confidence in them, it will be hard to apply them effectively to your own situation.

Principle 1: There is always another point of view

Our minds are capable of organising the same input in very different ways. To illustrate this principle have a look at the famous optical illusion below. What do you see?

Some of you will see an old lady with a beaked nose and a downcast gaze. Others will instantly recognise the illustration as that of a young woman with her head turned away from the viewer.

Keep looking and you will be able to make the image morph from one to the other, although it is not possible to 'see' both versions simultaneously. In selecting one interpretation our mind excludes the other.

So what has changed? Certainly not the illustration itself – the lines are fixed. It is our brain that organises the sensory information in different ways, yielding different interpretations of the picture that evoke very different responses in the observer.

> engrained habits in our thinking style predispose us towards 'seeing' the world in particular ways

CBT claims that a similar process takes place in the way we experience many aspects of our daily lives. There are engrained habits in our thinking style that predispose us towards 'seeing' the world in particular ways, and that encourage us to favour certain interpretations of events over others.

brilliant example

Anyone who doubts how differently the same events can affect people has only to look at footage of Barack Obama's election victory in November 2008. None celebrated harder than those who perceived the election of America's first black president as a landmark for civil rights. As a jubilant Oprah Winfrey announced to the world's media, 'It feels like hope won.'

However, this reaction could not have contrasted more strongly with that of the Republican supporters who had gathered at the Arizona Biltmore in time to hear John McCain concede defeat. The angry booing at the mention of Obama's name and the many disappointed, tearful faces bore witness to a very different perception of the night's results. As the Greek philosopher Epictetus remarked: 'Men are disturbed not by things, but by the view they take of them.'

Principle 2: Events *don't* cause our feelings

You have had the day from hell. You lost your car keys. Your boss shouted at you about filing that report late even though it wasn't your fault. Everyone went to the pub at lunchtime and for some reason you weren't invited. You return home to find the children are playing up and your wife in tears because the central heating has broken down. Is it any wonder you feel depressed, demoralised and overwhelmed? It's not difficult to see what made you feel that way.

But hold on. If the things that happen to us are responsible for our feelings how do we explain the fact that individuals react so differently to similar events? Why for one person does losing their car keys feel like a disaster, while for another the event is a minor inconvenience that is swiftly forgotten?

According to Beck, despite what we may assume, in themselves such events are not responsible for what we feel: rather it is our *interpretation* of events and the way we react to them that ultimately determines their impact upon our mood. This is a fundamental tenet of the cognitive behavioural approach.

Common sense may tell us that event A produces consequence B:

EVENT   REACTION

Loses car keys   ➡   Feels upset

However, CBT proposes there is always a crucial intermediate stage:

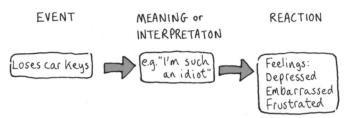

EVENT   MEANING or   REACTION
                     INTERPRETATON

Loses car keys ➡ e.g. "I'm such   ➡ Feelings:
                     an idiot"   Depressed
                                            Embarrassed
                                            Frustrated

Once we start recognising the importance of the meanings we assign we can quickly grasp how different readings of events carry such different emotional consequences.

exercise   **Match the feeling to the thought**

A man arranges to meet someone on a date. It is 10 minutes after the time agreed and his date still hasn't shown up. Look at the examples below and try to identify the emotional responses on the right that are most likely to accompany three contrasting interpretations of the same event.

Interpretation	Associated feelings	
1 'I'm not much of a catch – they probably decided not to bother coming...'	☐ Angry ☐ Disappointed ☐ Optimistic ☐ Bitter	☐ Composed ☐ Crestfallen ☐ Sad ☐ Anxious
2 'Typical: let down again! It just goes to show you can't trust anyone...'	☐ Angry ☐ Disappointed ☐ Optimistic ☐ Bitter	☐ Composed ☐ Crestfallen ☐ Sad ☐ Anxious
3 'They may well be stuck in traffic. They'll probably be here soon. If not maybe I'll take the opportunity to go and catch that movie I wanted to see.'	☐ Angry ☐ Disappointed ☐ Optimistic ☐ Bitter	☐ Composed ☐ Crestfallen ☐ Sad ☐ Anxious

These contrasting thoughts all carry a very different emotional tone. The first way of thinking is likely to leave the thinker feeling sad and forlorn and is typical of the thinking of a depressed person; while the second train of thought is more agitated, generating feelings of hostility and anxiety. It is pretty obvious that the third point of view is likely to generate less distress than either of the alternatives.

Principle 3: We all evolve characteristic ways of seeing the world

Although some ways of looking at events may leave us feeling better than others, surely people don't exercise much choice about the way they view situations or how they react emotionally? Many upsetting thoughts simply seem to pop into our heads unbidden – don't they? Aren't most of our responses just instinctive?

A cognitive behavioural therapist would completely agree with you. In fact Beck coined the term Negative Automatic Thoughts (NATs for short) to emphasise that much of the thinking responsible for our unwanted emotions is involuntary.

However this does not mean that it is not therefore possible to retrain the way we think. Indeed CBT aims to do just this, helping us 'change our minds' by unlearning unhelpful habits of thinking that can leave us at the mercy of unwanted emotions.

So how do these styles of thinking develop and become so entrenched? CBT points to two basic shaping processes – one that works from the outside in and a complementary process that works from the inside out.

How experience shapes our beliefs from the outside in

Events shape us. Indeed the behavioural element in CBT acknowledges its debt to a school of psychology – Behaviourism – that emphasised the way the brain forms associations in response to environmental input. What the early Behaviourists soon discovered, however, was that much more was going on than the blind pairing of stimulus and response: the rats in their mazes were actively learning. The results of some experiments simply didn't make sense unless the rats were creating internal maps of their world and automatically modifying them in response to new experiences.

Now depending on whose company you keep, you would probably agree that the average human being is more sophisticated than a rat. Our brains are remarkably good at searching for patterns. Human beings instinctively draw conclusions from their experiences all the time. If a child burns his hand on a stove he is unlikely to touch it again: he knows it is hot. However, not only is he unlikely to touch that particular stove, he will also approach any stove-like object he encounters in future with caution. His internal model of the world has been updated. We all generalise from our experience in ways that helpfully allow us to predict what might be coming up next.

> our brains are remarkably good at searching for patterns

Emotional learning is no different. A child who is neglected or abused may instinctively generate theories or even reach hard and fast conclusions about herself and the world around her: 'If I am being treated like this it must be because I am bad' or 'This person has hurt me... Other people will hurt me too'.

The layers of our belief system

We have already introduced NATs, the negative thoughts that spring unbidden into our minds and influence our emotional responses to things. However, our NATs are often closely linked to enduring assumptions we hold about ourselves and the world. These assumptions begin to form in childhood as we start to try to make sense of our experience. They make up a personal set of working theories about reality but they are not usually 'set in stone'. This is just as well because, as children, we often form our assumptions on the basis of limited life experience and inadequate evidence.

 **brilliant** insight

The formative years

Our internal models are very susceptible to input from other people, especially our parents. If you have been told throughout childhood that you are a capable, lovable individual you are likely to grow up seeing yourself that way. If you have been told you are 'an idiot' who will never amount to anything, these kinds of remarks will colour your assumptions about yourself and predispose you towards negative patterns of thought and feeling.

In CBT assumptions that are rigid, oppressive or narrow-minded, and that consequently end up making us unhappy, are usually referred to as *dysfunctional assumptions*. These often take the form of *conditional statements* (e.g. '*If* I do everything perfectly *then* I will be loved') or *moral imperatives* (e.g. 'I *must* never express my anger...', 'I *should* always put others before myself').

Dysfunctional assumptions represent the next layer down from NATs and tackling them in therapy can make a person much less vulnerable to a host of NATs that flow so readily from them.

Over time our experiences and assumptions gradually harden into our *core beliefs* – a set of fundamental position statements that we have intuitively distilled from our accumulated learning. Core beliefs can be much harder to pin down than NATs because they often take the form of *implicit* knowledge, only revealing themselves in our most generalised assumptions about ourselves, other people and the world around us.

Examples of destructive core beliefs

- 'I am a bad person.'
- 'Everyone is out for themselves.'
- 'I am not allowed to have anything good in my life.'
- 'The world is a dangerous place.'

They are the bedrock of our internal working model of the world and are usually strongly resistant (but not impossible) to change.

 insight

Sometimes once is enough!

If you want to teach a dog to come when you blow a whistle you will probably have to pair the whistle with a suitable reward many times. Classical conditioning theory states that the more often an outcome (the dog treat) is paired with a particular contingency (in this case coming at the whistle) the stronger that association will become. This is why childhood, with its strong repertoire of repeating patterns, is such a fertile breeding ground for our core assumptions.

However, after a single bad dose of food poisoning from a fish dish, psychologist John Seligman found that he couldn't stomach fish for a long time afterwards. Seligman realised that in some cases we only need to have one truly bad experience to alter our model of the world fundamentally.

It can be the same with events that unleash particularly powerful negative feelings – sometimes referred to by CBT therapists as *critical incidents*. Such events can make us jump to conclusions about ourselves and the world that can be hard to shake, even when unsupported by other evidence. Because they are associated with such threatening emotions we don't normally revisit or examine such beliefs.

How beliefs shape our perceptions from the inside out

We often filter out what doesn't fit with out existing beliefs

So far we have considered the way experience can shape how we see the world, but in CBT even more weight is given to the way that, once formed, our beliefs and assumptions can end up dictating the nature of our experience.

brilliant example

Imagine someone with strongly racist views reading a newspaper. On page 10 is an article reporting that the number of black youths arrested by the police in a particular district has doubled since last year. On page 13 is a story about an Asian man who ran into a burning building and rescued two children. Which of these two stories is likely to grab our racist reader's attention? How is he likely to respond when he reads that arrest rates correspond to an innovative local initiative persuading members of the community to volunteer information about teenage gang members using knives and other weapons? How will he explain the Asian man's motivation in rescuing the children? The reality is that our racist reader will probably enlist a combination of the sorts of strategies outlined below.

He will:

- **Discount or ignore information that does not fit with his preconceptions**. He might not bother to read the article about the fire rescue at all or skim quickly through the encouraging response to the new neighbourhood initiative.

- **Exaggerate elements from the reports that fit with his current views**. 'Unbelievable: now they've all got knives. No wonder crime rates in those black ghettos are soaring out of control...'

- **Explain away elements that don't fit with his beliefs as 'exceptions to the rule'**. 'You can bet your life most of those Pakis would just have let those poor kids burn...'

- **Attribute motivations that fit with current beliefs**. 'He probably only did it because he thought there might be a reward...'

Racial prejudice is an extreme case, but most of us resort to similar tactics in protecting our internal models of the world. Our assumptions and core beliefs often act as filters that block out anything that does not fit with our preconceptions. In Victor Hugo's famous novel *Les Misérables* the police inspector Javert eventually kills himself because of the unbearable conflict created in him by the altruistic and noble behaviour displayed by a man branded in his own mind as a criminal.

We may even find ourselves unconsciously seeking out experiences designed to reinforce our existing beliefs. This sort of mechanism operates when people go from one abusive relationship to the next. Sustained bad treatment at the hands of someone else is a surefire way to affirm hidden beliefs such as 'I am worthless', whereas allowing oneself to be loved properly within a healthy relationship might put real pressure on such a negative view.

Sadly we often cling to our belief system *even if those beliefs make us miserable*. Perhaps this is because 'knowing where we stand' – even if we convince ourselves that reality is very bleak – protects us against feeling lost and out of control. We are all creatures of habit. However, the techniques of CBT can help you prise open your grip on your assumptions and help you to challenge your own dysfunctional beliefs.

Principle 4: It's a two-way street

We have seen previously how certain thoughts appear to be capable of creating certain emotions: for example, if I think to myself 'I am ugly' then there is a good chance that such a thought might trigger feelings of shame, disgust or sadness. However CBT points out that the effect works both ways: in other words, if I am already feeling sad or depressed I am also much more likely to entertain thoughts associated with those emotions, in this case my 'ugly' thoughts.

This does not just apply to thoughts and feelings. The way we act can also predispose us to experience certain emotions or strengthen certain ways of thinking while particular moods or states of mind can encourage us to behave in a particular manner. For example, every time I avoid walking home a certain way because I know that a mugging took place there I reinforce my belief that the street is particularly dangerous and (because I don't go there anymore) I never have an experience that might alter that belief.

Our physiological reactions, which also count as 'behaviour' in CBT, can also cue powerful emotions and thoughts, but conversely emotions and thoughts can also directly affect our bodies.

My racing heartbeat and sweaty palms might provide all the evidence I need that 'something is seriously wrong with me' or 'I am having a heart attack'. These particular beliefs will inevitably also create a strong emotional reaction that may include feelings of fear and panic. The body's response to these emotions is to produce more adrenaline that, in turn, keeps the heart rate up, thereby 'proving' to the panicking person that something really *is* wrong. A feedback loop is established that just makes things worse.

This idea of mutual influence is really important because understanding these two-way, cause-and-effect relationships between symptoms can help us understand not only how problems become established, but also what keeps them going. CBT proposes that because our thoughts, feelings and behaviour are interconnected, changes in one area of the system will inevitably produce changes elsewhere.

Principle 5: We are all scientists at heart

You may not feel this one applies to you but, as we have seen, we are all theory-building creatures. We can't help ourselves. We are constantly generating hypotheses about ourselves and the world, often even without being aware that we are doing so.

Einstein and you... more in common than you might think?

Science is not all Higgs Bosons and Bunsen burners; more fundamentally it is a way of knowing things. Furthermore it is a way of knowing that has built-in quality assurance standards. In science a good theory or hypothesis has to meet at least two criteria:

1   it has to be consistent with all the available data, and

2   it can also be tested so we can find out whether it is trustworthy.

Even though we become very attached to our pet beliefs and may even distort our way of looking at things in order to defend them, ultimately CBT relies on the fact that we are not unreasonable: we need theories that fit with what we know of the world and that are able to make convincing sense of our lives. Cognitive behavioural therapy exploits this desire by encouraging us:

> ultimately CBT relies on the fact that we are not unreasonable

- to look at the way we may be distorting things to uphold our existing beliefs
- to become conscious of the underlying assumptions that steer our thoughts and reactions and treat them as provisional theories (hypotheses) rather than facts
- to test out the truth of our beliefs and assumptions against hard evidence from purpose-built behavioural experiments
- to conduct an objective review of *all* the relevant information available to see whether this data fits with our existing beliefs or whether those beliefs need to be changed.

In other words, CBT exploits the fact that, when it comes down to it, there are few of us who are not open to persuasion by a reasonable argument and the evidence of our own senses.

So now you know...

There you have it. You are now up to speed with the five funda-mental principles upon which CBT rests. They may look simple but, when applied in the right way, these ideas can provide a remarkably powerful set of insights. In the following chapter we will begin to explore how they can be mobilised to challenge some of the more common, negative thinking patterns.

CHAPTER 3

Common thinking traps – and how to avoid them

The philosopher Socrates was sitting outside the city gates of Athens when a man comes up to him. The man says: 'I am thinking of moving to Athens. What is it like living here?' Socrates looks up and asks him: 'I would gladly tell you but answer me one question: what is it like where you live now?' The man replied: 'Terrible! The people are back-stabbers and thieves. I will be leaving no friends behind me – only enemies.' Socrates frowned and replied, 'Well, you had best be on your way because you will only find the same thing here in Athens.'

Later a second man approached who was also considering moving to Athens. Once again the old philosopher asked him about his experience of his home town. The man smiled and said, 'Where I come from the people all work together and help each other. Kindness is everywhere and you are always treated with respect.' 'Welcome to Athens,' smiled Socrates, 'you will find the same thing here.'

Socrates knew that our mindset determines our experience of the world and he recognised that both men would carry their habitual attitudes, perceptions and ways of interacting with them. It was the way they processed information and biases in their thinking that were likely to dictate the quality of their lives just as much as the nature of their surroundings.

In order to escape from the mental prisons that we can so easily build for ourselves, CBT insists that we first need to become more aware of the biases in our thinking that can keep us trapped and unhappy. In this chapter we shall examine some of the most common thinking traps and help you become more aware of the ways in which they can perpetuate our difficulties. You will be given the opportunity to analyse your own thinking style and learn simple strategies for avoiding common thinking errors.

Thinking error 1: catastrophising

'The end of the world is nigh!'

'I can't find my purse... Oh no! I must have left it in the supermarket ... Someone is sure to have nicked it... Maybe it was stolen by someone who was looking over my shoulder when I got the money out of the cash dispenser in which case they know my PIN number and will probably already have emptied my bank account or stolen my identity... That means I won't be able to pay my bills this month... What if the bank decides to repossess the house? We'll be ruined. We're going to end up out on the street... How could I have been so stupid?'

We all know people who think like this. Catastrophising is the hallmark of an anxious person. It combines pessimism (i.e. assuming that in any situation a bad or distressing outcome is more likely than a good one) with a wildly exaggerated sense of threat. Things will not only be bad. They will be really bad.

Unfortunately people who catastrophise find it hard to appraise the significance of a situation realistically: they can end up becoming just as distressed by relatively trivial setbacks as a major misfortune. They constantly project themselves into a doom-laden future and allow their imaginations to run riot with frightening scenarios.

People who catastrophise seldom take into account any resources they might have to deal with the worst-case scenario. If this is you ask yourself:

- On the scale of all the bad things that have happened in the past or could happen to you in the future, how bad could this event be?
- If I had no choice but to deal with the very worst thing that could happen in this situation what would I actually do?
- Think about how you may have dealt with other past difficulties. What helped you then?

Thinking error 2: generalisation

'Things *always* go wrong for me...'

Human beings are drawn to patterns. We frequently use our experience as a template for our predictions about the future. However, people who are inclined to generalise require little evidence in order to deduce laws and assumptions about the way the world works – and invariably their observations and deductions are pretty downbeat. A man loses a game of Scrabble and thinks to himself 'Typical! I never win at anything.' A young girl gets teased at school and concludes, 'Everyone hates me!' An elderly lady reads about a mugging in the local paper and ruefully concludes that 'No one is safe these days...'. All of these are examples of generalisation in which an individual draws some far-reaching, universal conclusion on the basis of a single unpleasant experience or discrete piece of information.

The language of people prone to generalisation is usually a reliable giveaway. If you hear yourself using absolute terms like '*never*', '*always*', '*everyone*' and '*no one*' a lot, then the chances are you may be vulnerable to this type of thinking.

In order to counter generalisation you need to train yourself to look for exceptions to your own rules. If you have one friend in the world then it is not the case that 'no one' likes you and it is highly unlikely you have 'never' won at anything – even if your distorted thinking probably makes it hard for you to bring any past victories to mind. The danger with generalisations is that we tend to screen out anything that does not correspond with our ill-founded convictions, whereas we eagerly seize upon fresh evidence that appears to support our negative beliefs about ourselves and others.

> we eagerly seize upon fresh evidence that appears to support our negative beliefs

Unfortunately, generalisations easily become self-fulfilling prophecies. For example, someone who believes she is universally unpopular will make little effort to make herself amenable to other people.

Thinking error 3: mind reading

'She thinks I am an idiot'

We make assumptions about other people and their intentions all the time. To some extent this is necessary, and we can reliably infer a great deal from people's actions and past behaviour towards us. However, in some circumstances our imaginations run riot. We leap to conclusions about other people's motives and attitudes on the basis of very little hard evidence. We are especially inclined to do this when those motives and attitudes affect us directly.

The trouble is that when we make these kinds of assumptions we leave ourselves open to all kinds of misunderstandings and paranoid projections. The fact of the matter is that we have no way of knowing for certain what another person is thinking unless they choose to tell us.

brilliant example

One of the interventions often recommended to CBT clients prone to mind reading involves consulting other people regarding their views and perceptions.

A young male client who was sent away with the homework task of asking his family and friends what they valued about him made every excuse under the sun to avoid having to complete the assignment. He would feel self-conscious. He wouldn't be able to get hold of some of the relevant people. He didn't have the time because of the pressure of his college work. Before his session the following week I half expected him to turn up claiming that the dog had eaten his homework sheets.

Nevertheless, when Paul did arrive for his session we were both pleasantly surprised by the results. Not only had he completed the task and interviewed the people as suggested, but reported that he had been both moved and secretly delighted by some of the compliments he had been paid.

Paul confessed that he had been terrified of conducting these enquiries because he had been convinced that even the people closest to him perceived him as 'an annoying nerd'. This wasn't actually the case, but because of this entrenched belief Paul had never risked testing out the reality of the situation. Relying instead on his highly developed 'mind reading' powers, Paul had laboured under an unnecessary assumption that was eating away at his self-esteem.

Thinking error 4: polarised and rigid thinking

'It's black or white...'

'It's right or it's wrong', 'You're a winner or loser', 'If it's not the best then it's rubbish…'. People who tend to think all the time in these kind of dichotomies are likely to create all kinds of problems for themselves psychologically. The world is just not that simple. Our classifications are always imperfect, and trying to force reality into convenient boxes seldom works very well.

Think about weight for example. Polarised thinking would insist that if you are not thin you must therefore be fat. This ignores the fact that if you lined the population of London up in a line there would be little agreement on the point at which the 'skinny' people ended and the 'overweight' people began.

Obesity is a good example of a continuum concept with a rather arbitrary cut off. It's also a cultural construct – a social judgement rather than an objective truth.

Polarised and rigid thinking often goes hand in hand with strong moral judgements and self-evaluations that can cause a great deal of unnecessary distress. You may also have noticed that polarised or dogmatic thinkers usually spend a great deal of time trying to impose their own classification system on other people. Their moral absolutism tolerates no dissent – after all, in their eyes there is only one right way. Unfortunately this kind of polarised thinking leads to a great many evils in society including racism, bigotry, sexism and political extremism. Often people who think in rigid ways put themselves and others under a great deal of unnecessary pressure.

People who think in extremes have few places to go. It is no coincidence that CBT places so much emphasis on softening the absolutes in our thinking and encouraging us to think more flexibly. This is not about ditching your values or becoming an amoral person. It is simply about recognising that people can see and experience things in different ways, and that more flexible, sophisticated ways of perceiving are likely to be better for your mental health.

> people who think in extremes have few places to go

brilliant tip

Think in terms of sliding scales

People often complain that CBT places an unnecessary emphasis on percentages, ratings and measurements. However, recognising that, when it comes to levels of conviction or the degrees of emotion we feel, we are always at some point on a sliding scale creates the possibility of moving up and down in either direction. If there are only two opposites to choose from, then shifting from one position to the other often becomes a daunting task. Moving a few inches in either direction is a much less intimidating and more realistic prospect.

Here are a few suggestions:

- Watch out for terms in your speech and thinking such as 'should', 'ought to' and 'must' that may indicate the presence of unhelpfully rigid assumptions about yourself and the world:
  - 'Women *should* always obey their husbands.'
  - 'I *must* always put others first.'
  - 'Children *should* be seen and not heard.'
- Try to embrace the grey: recognise that many concepts are better conceptualised as a sliding scale rather than a choice between stark alternatives.
- Learn to see your values and convictions as a matter of personal choice rather than obligatory for everyone.
- Expose yourself to other views that don't necessarily fit in with your own and see if you can find any common ground with those who hold them.

Thinking error 5: emotional reasoning

'I feel so guilty... I must have done something awful'

Albert Ellis, the American psychologist and psychotherapist, talked about 'thought-feeling fusion' by which he meant that our cognitive and emotional responses are often two aspects of the same thing. Usually in CBT we are looking for the negative thoughts that prime distressing emotions, but it is important to recognise that our feelings can also encourage us along certain lines of thought. Sometimes our strong feelings can be treated as 'evidence' for the truth of our negative thoughts. This is called emotional reasoning and it can get us into all kinds of trouble.

 **example**

'He's really winding me up!' This is a common complaint in my household. What it often means is that one of my children is feeling stressed and frustrated by the other and therefore assumes that the other has deliberately behaved in a way to produce this effect. The reality is that often this is not the case: the impact of the behaviour is unintentional, but the level of irritation the 'victim' is experiencing makes any other more innocent explanation seem impossible. We have to take great care not to let the emotions we feel function as evidence for the truth of our beliefs.

The following are common examples of emotional reasoning:

I *feel* attacked   →   'Someone must be getting at me...'
I *feel* guilty   →   'I must have done something bad...'
I *feel* scared   →   'Something awful is about to happen.'

The antidote to emotional reasoning is to recognise that our emotions are not reliable guides when it comes to establishing facts. Often our emotions cloud our judgement or act as a field of static that make it hard for us to see things clearly.

- Recognise that your emotions are not necessarily accurate guides when it comes to establishing the truth.
- Set your feelings to one side and consider what hard evidence there may be that supports your conclusions.
- Consider other possible explanations.
- Ask yourself: 'Would someone else be reacting to this situation in the same way?'

Thinking error 6: blaming

'It's all *your* fault'

On the whole blame is a pretty counterproductive pastime. The task of dishing out responsibility for what has happened can preoccupy people in a way that effectively disengages their problem-solving abilities. When the situation is 'someone else's fault' then there is little call to do anything further about it, let alone seek to understand the role that one's own behaviour, feelings or assumptions might have played in bringing the problem about. Blame is a dead end cognitively and a sure-fire cue for a whole host of destructive emotions such as resentment, bitterness, anger and hatred.

> blame is a dead end cognitively and a sure-fire cue for a whole host of destructive emotions

Often blaming others is a defensive manoeuvre for people who are unable to tolerate the possibility that they might be at fault in some way. By now you will probably recognise that this fear of being flawed is because of a distorted sense of how bad it would be to be less than perfect. Scratch the surface of someone inclined to blame others and you will often unearth dysfunctional assumptions such as 'I must be perfect and good at all times or people will hate me' (catastrophising) or 'If I am not perfect then I am useless and unworthy' (polarised thinking).

There are some people who err on the other side and have a tendency to make *themselves* overly responsible for the bad things that happen to them and others.

People who suffer from Obsessive Compulsive Disorder (OCD) – a condition in which people attempt to reduce their anxiety by performing rituals like washing or making unusual mental rules for themselves – are particularly prone to self-blame.

Their sense of how awful it would be if they did cause harm often appears to convince them that they have or could, even in magical and implausible ways.

One teenage girl I worked with was convinced that if she did not switch off her bedroom light in the right way some terrible illness or accident would befall the people she loved. I knew another woman who was convinced that germs she might have transferred to a letter were going to make the recipient's baby sick. She fretted about this constantly and became so obsessed with the idea that she was unable to sleep at night.

These kind of examples are extreme, and may seem bizarre to anyone who does not suffer from OCD. However, we can all demonstrate a tendency to make ourselves responsible for things that may only partially be within our control or even completely beyond it. The tell-tale emotion of self-blame is guilt. When we do cause distress to others guilt is a natural and appropriate emotion, but if you feel guilty a lot of the time for no very good reason then this could be an indication that a distorted sense of overdeveloped responsibility or a very negative set of core beliefs may be controlling your life.

Thinking error 7: filtering and magnifying

'You see! It's just as I thought...'

This is an almost universal thought distortion of which we are all guilty at times. Filtering, as the name suggests, is when we only attend to information that fits with our preconceptions and disregard other equally legitimate information. Magnifying is when we exaggerate the importance or frequency of events that fit with our current beliefs.

 **brilliant** example

Jane is organising a wedding for her best friend. In the middle of the reception it becomes apparent that the caterers have mixed up the orders and sent vol-au-vents rather than the blinis with salmon and cream cheese that were requested.

Jane is horrified. As far as she is concerned it just goes to prove that the job of organising the wedding should have been entrusted to someone more competent. Today was supposed to be perfect and now she has let her friend down. In fact she is sure she caught her looking slightly teary when she found out.

Of course the friend tried to make her feel better, saying that it didn't matter at all, but Jane knew in her heart that the special day hadn't gone the way her friend wanted and felt mortified. She had failed again and it just went to prove that everything her mother always said about her was right all along.

It is clear that Jane is a past master at both filtering and magnifying. She ignores completely the many things that have gone according to plan on her friend's big day and focuses entirely on the one minor detail that didn't.

The reason she does so is because she is unconsciously looking for evidence to support her core belief, 'I am no good', and in order to do so she has to screen out the abundant evidence of her success as a wedding planner, concentrating exclusively on her one 'failure' – even though the mix-up was not even her fault.

She works hard to inflate both the significance of the wrong canapés and the bride's reaction: note that Jane does not ascribe her friend's possible tearfulness to the joy of the whole occasion or any other cause. She also has to convince herself that her friend's reassurance is based entirely on an altruistic desire to make Jane feel better, not that she genuinely might not care about the vol-au-vent switch. Jane also superimposes her own assumption that the day has to be 'perfect' in order to make the mistake all the more terrible. No wonder she is distraught.

To prevent yourself going down the same road:

- Try to see the whole picture – take into account *all* the facts, even if they don't seem to fit with your expectations.
- See whether you can build a case for the *opposite* of what you currently believe: in our example that the wedding was a runaway success and that Jane did an exceptional job.
- Check that you are not blowing certain elements out of proportion. Did other people react in the same way as you did?

Thinking error 8: emotive language

Words are powerful things, and certain words have an emotional resonance that can colour our thinking – often in unhelpful ways. We can describe events to ourselves in terms that can either inflame our reactions or calm them down.

If I tell myself, 'That man *despises* everything I stand for,' rather than, 'We don't always see eye to eye' I will instantly feel on the defensive next time we meet. If I say to myself that a situation was '*utterly humiliating*' as opposed to 'briefly uncomfortable' I will be making strenuous efforts to avoid similar situations in future – even if such protective manoeuvres are entirely unnecessary. My language has effectively raised the stakes.

Emotive language is one of the main reasons why people end up convincing themselves that they will be unable to tolerate situations that they have perfectly adequate resources to cope with:

- 'It would be the *worst thing* if people laughed at my performance. I would look like such an *idiot*'.
- 'I *wouldn't be able to live with myself* if anything happened to her.'
- 'It would be *simply awful* to end up alone... .'

Be careful that when you describe past or future events to yourself you do not prejudice yourself: this is counterproductive.

It is very hard to think objectively about a scenario that has already been given a strong emotional inflection and it is often our language that colours our perceptions and feeds our anxieties and low moods.

- When thinking or talking about emotionally inflammatory scenarios check your vocabulary and make sure you are not throwing fuel on the fire of your negative thoughts.
- Strive to achieve the most neutral, objective tone that you can.
- When recalling distressing events imagine that you are writing a bulletin for a news broadcast that requires you to assume a detached, objective perspective.

 **exercise** How brilliant are you at spotting thinking errors?

The following quiz is designed to see whether you can use your knowledge to identify which common thinking errors are being committed in these examples. Remember, you are looking for cases of the following:

- catastrophising
- polarised 'black and white' thinking
- rigid thinking
- excessive self-blame
- unrealistic blame of others
- filtering
- magnifying
- mind reading
- emotive language.

Be aware that some of these thinking errors are not mutually exclusive and you may find more than one in the same example.

▶

Also, as you run through the list try to speculate about the emotions that might be associated with the type of thoughts and behaviours described. (The answers are on page 57.)

1   A man is invited to a party to celebrate a colleague's recent promotion. He crumples the invite and chucks it in the bin. He thinks: 'Joel must be feeling pretty pleased with himself now that all his scheming has paid off. Ever since he arrived he has been making trouble and trying to edge me out. Look at the way he struck up that friendship with the supervisor – what a reptile! I can still hear the sarcasm dripping from his voice when he said how "sorry" he was that I didn't get enough recognition for the Johnson deal. I bet he has been spreading all kinds of lies and rumours about me. Of course this means I will probably never get promoted and I will spend the rest of my life pushing paper in this bloody dead-end job.'

2   I wake up and feel a bit off colour. My immediate thoughts run as follows: 'Not good... not good. I haven't felt okay for a few days now – perhaps there's something seriously wrong with me... Come to think of it my legs feel really heavy and my hand was shaking the other day when I was reading that tax bill. I know Jill thinks it's just because I have been working really late and I'm a bit run down but what if it's multiple sclerosis? I know that someone on my mother's side had MS. Oh God! Now I can feel these weird tingling sensations in my fingers. What's happening to me?'

3   'There's just no excuse for behaviour like that... The way she spoke to you was simply unforgivable. We have always had Christmas at your mother's. It's a family tradition. What was she thinking? Young people are all the same: no respect for their elders.'

4 'If she says no I know I just won't be able to cope. I would be so embarrassed. I'm going to make a fool of myself and it will all be for nothing. Why would she want to go to the dance with me anyway? I am sure she would much rather go with Kieran... She probably only said she liked me because she felt sorry for me.'

5 'Everything's ruined. I've just made a complete mess of things. I just played one wrong note after another and I know I cocked up the rhythm in that middle section completely. They all expected me to get a distinction and I barely managed to scrape a merit. They are going to be so disappointed in me. Maybe I should give up the piano altogether. What's the point in struggling on when I obviously don't have any talent for it?'

Homework: getting personal

Over the next week keep a record of your upsetting thoughts. Carry a notebook with you and write them down as soon as you can, using the same phrasing and images that run through your mind at the time.

Once you have collected a good sized sample of your thinking go carefully through your log and see whether you can find evidence of the kind of thinking errors described in this chapter. Once you become aware of the cognitive habits that may be strengthening your negative thought patterns it becomes much easier to start breaking them.

Answers: 1) mind reading, filtering, emotive language, blaming, magnifying, catastrophising; 2) magnifying, filtering, catastrophising and emotive language catastrophising; 3) generalisation, polarised thinking, rigid thinking, emotive language; 4) emotive language, catastrophising; 5) emotive language, generalisation, polarised thinking, filtering, magnifying, mind-reading.

CHAPTER 4

Grappling with negative thinking

So you have grasped the basic principle of CBT. You know your NATs from your core beliefs and are getting better at spotting both. You can even recognise common thinking errors and traps. By this stage you will be all too aware of the power of your thoughts to twist reality into forms that can upset, frighten or depress you. You recognise that although it may well be appropriate to experience such feelings from time to time, if you are experiencing such emotions on a regular basis then the chances are your habitual ways of thinking are probably at fault.

Fortunately, because these ways of thinking offer an unrealistic or warped perception of the world they are also vulnerable to reason. Your powers of rationality are one of the main weapons you have at your disposal when countering negative thinking, but like all weapons, you need to learn how to wield them effectively. This chapter will show you how to get started.

You may be thinking to yourself that 'rationality' and 'reason' aren't necessarily your strong point? Perhaps you see yourself as more of a 'gut feeling', intuitive type? Don't be put off. In this case brilliance is not mandatory. To use these techniques requires neither the incisive logic of Spock or the analytical prowess of a chess grandmaster. A willingness to think things through and a good dose of common sense should see you right. Remember, deep down even the most flighty of us like things to make sense, and it is this drive that CBT harnesses in countering dysfunctional thinking. So how on earth do we go about reprogramming our thinking?

Look for exceptions to the rule

Strictly speaking, if something is true then it must be compatible with *all* the available evidence. Consequently, one of the basic cognitive procedures in taking a negative thought to task is to trawl for any information or experiences that might contradict your unhelpful belief.

You are at a social event feeling tongue-tied and awkward. Negative thinking may be telling you 'I never have anything interesting to say', but hold on a minute: what about that dinner party when you kept everyone enthralled for the best part of half an hour with your amusing anecdotes about your time in Nepal? And what about the friends who seek out your company on a regular basis? If you really had nothing to say would they keep coming back for more? And didn't Jane comment that you had been missed at the recent book club meeting because of your original views?

Now of course your negative mind will swiftly cut in and try to disqualify these apparent anomalies. This is because if there is any substance to any of your examples then the claim 'I *never* have anything interesting to say' starts to look a bit shaky. The more contradictory examples you can pull up, the weaker the NAT becomes. What your counter-evidence suggests is that you have fallen prey to the thinking errors of *filtering* and *generalisation*. Once you realise this you can start to negotiate a more reasonable alternative position: 'I have lots to say but it takes me a while to feel confident when meeting new people'. This feels a lot less damning and is actually more accurate.

the more contradictory examples you can pull up, the weaker the NAT becomes

 **brilliant** tip

Keep it real

Remember: Your alternative thoughts must always be believable. There is no point just trying to deny your NATs by defiantly asserting that the opposite is true. You need to find a balanced position that feels realistic. There is no point replacing one distortion with another: 'I am the best at everything I do' is not an appropriate counter to the core belief 'I am hopeless at everything I do' because it is unlikely to convince you or anyone else. An alternative position such as 'no one is good at everything but there are *many* things I do well' is a much more potent response – especially if it is based on a conscientious and level-headed review of examples of your various skills and talents.

The most powerful challenges to our negative beliefs are usually those drawn from our own experience, which is why behavioural experiments play such a key role in CBT – but more of that in the next chapter. However, information from trusted sources can also provide us with useful ammunition at times. For example, for some people who are phobic about flying it does make a difference to learn that the accident statistics confirm that there really is more chance of dying crossing the road than in an aircraft crash.

If your response to this is something along the lines of 'That's all very well but I feel I have more control when I cross the road...', then you may just have tapped into an underlying dysfunctional assumption ('*I must feel in control in every situation...*') that may be making flying – and a bunch of other experiences – difficult for you.

Give your 'but' a workout

In sessions when you present someone with a piece of evidence that doesn't fit with their negative thoughts there is one small word you will hear with great frequency: 'but'.

> *Therapist* Inga, you tell me that you are not academic but what about this 'A' that you got on your latest assignment? That doesn't sound like the grade of someone who is, I quote, 'rubbish at studying'?

> *Inga:* But you see, it's only because I was able to borrow my friend's lecture notes – he's just got a really clear way of presenting stuff because he understands it – unlike me.

Our instinctive and irrational drive to defend our negative thoughts means that we all too swiftly find reasons and excuses to dismiss the information that doesn't fit, but this is actually a tactic that can be used *against* your NATs and dysfunctional assumptions.

Collect the evidence that supports your negative thought and then systematically work through it, using the word 'but' as your cue to find loopholes and exemption clauses that might discredit the evidence.

 **example**

Negative thought: *'I am going to make a complete idiot of myself when I get onstage tonight.'*

Evidence supporting the negative thought		Qualifier/excuse
Time when I couldn't read out loud in class because I felt like I couldn't breathe. Everyone laughed.	*BUT...*	I did have undiagnosed asthma and I've got an inhaler now.

Evidence supporting the negative thought		Qualifier/excuse
I'm not confident in front of groups...	**BUT...**	I can be quite outspoken and assertive when I really believe in something.
I'll probably forget my lines at some point.	**BUT...**	Sally is there to act as prompt and it's a pantomime. I can always ad lib a bit.

Remember, as any defence lawyer knows, if you can undermine the foundations of a witness's testimony then you can do serious damage to their plausibility. Taking apart the evidence for your automatic thoughts or even core assumptions piece by piece can sometimes be enough to bring the whole edifice tumbling down.

Aim at the right target

Sometimes people fail to make much impact on their problems because they attempt to do battle with the surface thoughts rather than the more damaging assumptions and implications behind them. This is a bit like trying to control a cholera epidemic without paying attention to the cracked sewerage system and polluted water supply.

brilliant example

Dinah is preparing a birthday party for her son Luke. She takes the cake out of the oven to find that it has risen unevenly and feels a wave of panic sweep over her while the negative thought plays through her mind: 'Oh my god! Now everything's ruined!' She could, of course, use the techniques we have been discussing to dispute this thought:

▶

- Many things in her life and even her son's party will remain completely unchanged by this so-called culinary 'disaster'.
- Judging from previous experience the children will probably not even notice if the cake is uneven.
- Even the cake is not technically 'ruined' because she knows full well she can disguise the sunken section with extra butter cream.

However, even though she is applying appropriate counters Dinah finds that these alternative thoughts make little impression on her low mood. The reason for this is that she has not delved sufficiently deeply into the assumptions underlying her mood shift. Had she pushed herself a little further she would swiftly have uncovered the immediate source of her anxiety, namely the belief that *'everything I do has to be perfect'*.

Dinah could have unearthed this dysfunctional assumption by using a technique known in CBT as the *downward arrow*. Put simply this means that when you hit a negative thought you ask yourself 'What does this mean about me or the world?' or 'What is the worst implication of this?' and you repeat the process until you hit the appropriate 'hot' thought. If Dinah had used the downward arrow technique the results would have looked something like this:

Now everything is ruined

                    Which means/matters because...

It's not as I planned

                    Which means/matters because...

I've messed things up

     Which means/matters because...

I must ensure everything is perfect

     Which means/matters because...

People will be disappointed in me

     Which means/matters because...

I won't be loved

The thought that actually provoked Dinah's anxiety was the dysfunctional assumption '*I must ensure everything I do is perfect... or I won't be loved*'. This was the thought that she needed to be challenging, so in her case the following counters would probably have proved more effective:

- I have made mistakes in the past such as when I reversed the car into that bollard. My husband was just relieved that I was okay. My foul-up didn't seem to make any difference to how he felt about me. Luke probably won't love me any the less if the cake is a bit lopsided for once.

- Other people make mistakes and are still lovable. Uncle Henry did terrible things and everyone still adored him so maybe my assumption isn't always true.

- There is a respected school of thought that people should be loved for who they are, not what they do.

brilliant tip

The jury is out!

Some people get despondent because they cannot ever imagine themselves not believing their negative thought. One strategy that can help is to cast yourself into the role of a lawyer. Solicitors and barristers don't take on their cases on the basis of whether they believe their client to be guilty or innocent. Their job is to represent one side of the argument to the best of their ability. The weighing of the relative merits of the arguments comes later down the line when the jury considers its verdict. At this stage you do not have to convince yourself of anything – merely commit yourself to examining the available evidence in an unbiased way and make the best case you can for revising your current belief.

Stand it on its head

Sometimes the best way to expose the weakness of a negative thought is not to contradict it directly but to examine the *opposite* of the thought. This can be an especially productive strategy to adopt with dysfunctional assumptions.

brilliant example

Peter has OCD and a host of anxious thoughts about cleanliness and infection. He is standing at the kitchen sink having just washed up a chopping board when it occurs to him that it may not be entirely clean. He washes it again. And again. And again. Each time he does so his negative thoughts become stronger and his anxiety levels escalate. The thought that keeps playing through his head is this one:

Peter's NAT: *'If I don't wash this one more time I cannot be sure all the germs are gone.'*

Using this technique Peter inverts his original thought:

Peter's inverted assumption: *'If I **do** wash this one more time I **can** be sure that all the germs have gone.'*

As soon as he put it to himself in these terms Peter realises this is nonsense. His new thought – although simply an inversion of his original one – no longer felt convincing. He was then able to dispute the new thought using the following counters:

* *Even if I wash this board a thousand times I will never know for sure that all the germs have been removed.*

* *New germs may be falling on the board all the time – and there is nothing I can do about that because I can't keep washing it for ever.*

Once the whole enterprise had convincingly been exposed as pointless, Peter was finally able to abandon his obsessive cleansing ritual for the time being. It didn't deliver him from his anxiety because he was not quite ready to challenge his entrenched beliefs that things needed to be sterile if he and other people were to avoid contamination. However, the futility of his actions did put a break on a behaviour that was inevitably reinforcing his problems.

Inverting your NATs and seeing whether the *opposite* holds true can be a helpful starting point. The transformed NAT may feel outlandish, but the mirror image won't carry the negative emotional charge of the original. This means you may find yourself able to examine it more objectively.

> seeing whether the *opposite* holds true can be a helpful starting point

If I am telling myself that 'nobody loves me...' I may find it hard to appraise such a thought rationally. The inverted form – '*everybody* loves me' – is, of course, also grossly inaccurate, but considering the arguments 'for' and 'against' may allow me to recall one or two people who do care about me. Neither of the polarised extremes are correct, but while the first may be paralysing, its mirror image may be more open to objective evaluation. Evidence from that process can then be carried over to dispute the original NAT:

New counter: '*I feel unloved at the moment but there is good evidence that* **some** *people in the world have cared about me and absolutely no reason to believe that they do not continue to do so.*'

See the situation through fresh eyes

A great many of the beliefs that seem self-evident to us are not so obvious to other people. One simple but surprisingly effective technique you can employ to counter your negative beliefs is to ask yourself how the situation would appear to someone else and check whether they would agree with your conclusions.

Fred can't get to sleep. Yesterday he forgot to ring his mate Steve on his birthday and he is rapidly convincing himself that he has jeopardised the friendship. However, by putting himself into the shoes of Chris, a mutual and more laid-back friend, he is able to use Chris's perspective to answer some of his own NATs.

Fred's negative thoughts	The 'Chris' take on the situation
What I've done is unforgivable...	That's a bit strong. It's an easy mistake to make – and Steve is a really understanding guy. That's partly why we both like him. I forget stuff all the time. What are you getting so worked up about?
He won't ever want to see or speak to me again.	You're his best friend – wouldn't that be cutting off his nose to spite his face?
How could I be so stupid?	Don't give yourself such a hard time. You've had so much on your plate this week what with your dad's operation and your brother's arrest. Steve knows that.
I don't deserve to have a good friend like Steve.	Isn't it up to Steve to decide who he wants to be mates with? Anyway you've been a good friend to him: it was you that got him through the whole ugly divorce with Angie.

Since many of our negative thoughts involve our critical self-perceptions it can be particularly useful to choose as your alternative viewpoint someone who you know cares about you and is sympathetic towards you. What this technique encourages you to do is *de-centre* or step outside your own restricted perceptions by accessing parts of your mind not necessarily held hostage to your negative assumptions. If you are finding this approach a struggle why not actually ask a friend or loved one for real? It can be an eye-opener.

Ask yourself: 'How did I come to believe this in the first place?'

When in the grip of a negative thought process our instinctive response to this question might be, 'Because it's true, of course!': but the origins of our beliefs are usually based in specific experiences that have taught us to think in certain ways.

When addressing a negative thought, can you identify any critical incidents or experiences responsible for the current levels of your conviction regarding your belief? If you had not been through that experience would that have changed the way you see things?

Maybe your belief is a piece of received wisdom, a piece of programming handed down from someone close to you. When you think about your belief can you picture anyone else who shares it? Is this something you can remember someone else saying to you? Was it an explicit or implicit message repeated in your childhood? This of course does not necessarily mean that the belief is invalid but you might want to scrutinise it carefully to see whether it holds true. Critical experiences and repeated childhood patterns can mould our core beliefs about ourselves in various ways. We will return to the topic of core beliefs and how you tackle them later in this chapter.

For now, be reassured that the very process of thinking about your thinking – called *metacognition* by the psychologists – is valuable, because in order to do so you have to take a step back. Sometimes this is all that is needed to bring about a perceptual shift and make our negative thoughts seem less compelling.

How helpful is this belief?

CBT is a pragmatic business. Its focus is results – results measured against the targets that you have set for yourself. When we think of problems it is usual to think of them as something we want to resolve or move away from, but CBT encourages you to think more positively than this. It would ask you to reflect upon the state that you wish to move *towards*. This may seem like a subtle distinction but it is an important one. In CBT you don't only evaluate your negative thoughts on the basis of how true they are: you will also be considering how *useful* they are in terms of achieving your goals.

reflect upon the state that you wish to move towards

Say, for example, that my problem is that I am agoraphobic – in other words I have found myself feeling increasingly unsafe in crowded places. I have set myself the following goal:

Goal: *To be able to get out and about without feeling afraid so I can live a full and active social life again.*

I go to the cupboard to get some bread to make toast for breakfast but find that I have used the last of the loaf. I briefly consider nipping to the local bakery which is a five-minute walk from the house, but as I do so a terrible sense of foreboding starts to gnaw away in the pit of my stomach. I start shaking and feeling unsteady. Because I have dutifully worked my way through the preceding chapters of this book I begin to become conscious of a stream of negative thinking. In particular I picture myself panicking in the bakers and drawing attention to myself by acting in an eccentric, 'crazy' fashion. I think to myself:

Question: *If I am to become someone who can get out and about without feeling afraid is this image helpful to me?*

Answer: *Absolutely not. All it does is make me more afraid. It is completely incompatible with my goal so I need to either get rid of it or modify it.*

Question: *When I have achieved my goal of conquering my agoraphobia then what image will I have in my head in these circumstances?*

Answer: *I probably wouldn't dwell on it and just grab my keys and go. But if I did stop to anticipate it I would picture myself walking cheerfully into the bakers, possibly meeting someone I know, calmly buying my bread and walking home again.*

While mentally rehearsing this alternative vision of the trip I notice that my hands have stopped shaking so much. Although my anxiety has certainly not gone away, it would appear that this new vision of myself buying bread has the potential to move things in the desired direction. One image intensifies and consolidates my symptoms, the alternative brings me a little more into alignment with my goal. There is little question as to which I should consciously embrace if I want to progress towards an anxiety-free future.

Asking yourself how you will think about things once the problem has gone and trying it on for size is another way of opening up alternative perspectives that can loosen the hold of even the pernicious NAT.

Say it *is* so... What can you do about it?

One of the chief difficulties with negative thoughts of all kinds is their capacity to paralyse us and leave us feeling helpless.

They usually come with an unspoken implication which reads, in effect, '...and there is nothing you can do about it!'

- *I am such a jealous person...* [and you're stuck like that].
- *I just don't have the energy to get my act together...* [so there's no point trying really].
- *I never have been popular* [and never will...].

Often what you need to dispute is not the validity of the thought itself, but the truth of this invisible corollary – that you are completely helpless in the situation. In most cases there certainly *is* something you can do about the scenario painted by your negative mindset, often many things. One of the most effective ways to counter negative thinking is to approach your NATs as cues to start problem solving. Even if you currently find it impossible to accept that your distorted view of reality is right, there is nothing to prevent you from doing something about it.

Your negative thoughts tell you that you have no friends. So rather than colluding with this thought by getting really miserable and brooding on your isolation, you make a list of three things you could do to start changing that:

1 Ring up the bloke who gave you his number after the match last Saturday and see whether he wants to go for that drink.

2 Open up a Facebook account and find out what your old mates from school are up to.

3 Go to that office party next week rather than sitting glumly at home as usual and make an effort to be a bit more sociable.

The joy of this approach is that before long you will probably have a number of new experiences that will arm you to dispute future negative thoughts in a similar vein.

Once more with feeling!

Sometimes people find that even once they have achieved a more balanced position and are no longer logically convinced of the truth of a negative thought it continues to exercise power over their mood. This is actually not surprising.

Firstly, while we do sometimes have flashes of insight and revelation that transform our worldview and lift the scales from our eyes, such incidents are the exception rather than the rule. It's easy to see why.

For a start your negative beliefs have probably been rehearsed and reinforced over a very long period. At a physical level, the pathways in our brains get strengthened the more times we use them. In particular, thought processes relating to core beliefs will inevitably have been reinforced assiduously over many years. A new and consequently more fragile neural trace (your alternative thought) will need to be strengthened by constant repetition before it begins to take hold. In short, reprogramming your thinking involves running the new programme many times before it becomes spontaneous, natural and convincing. Be prepared to repeat the new thought to yourself again and again.

> be prepared to repeat the new thought to yourself again and again

The other reason why alternative thoughts sometime fail to control our negativity is that we don't mobilise them with sufficient oomph! Our NATs already come with a pre-set emotional charge. In fact it is their power to mobilise our emotions that partly defines them and gives them their hold over us. However, if we are to establish the supremacy of a new position then this needs to be applied with equal and opposite emotional force, even if it is the product of 'cooler' processes like logic and reason.

When you superimpose your new alternative belief over your old one be assertive! Imagine you are delivering it with the force of a knock-out blow. Mentally shout it out – if you are hesitant or tentative the underlying implication is that you don't have much faith in your new perspective. Think it like you mean it. If you can bear it, it can really help to actually say it out loud with as much vocal conviction as you can muster. Sometimes I encourage clients to write their alternative thoughts on a piece of paper next to the bathroom mirror and repeat them every morning five times at the start of the day. You may feel self-conscious but it does help.

Working with thought records

If you are serious about tackling your issues, the mundane reality is that when you start countering your dysfunctional thought patterns you will be filling in a lot of thought records. This stage will not go on for ever, but really is worthwhile for a number of reasons:

- Thought records teach you to dispute your NATs in a systematic and methodical fashion.
- They will provide feedback in the form of mood ratings so you can see how you are doing.
- They will help you work towards more balanced, realistic alternative thoughts by synthesising the evidence for and against your automatic thoughts.
- The very act of writing your thoughts and feelings down will give you a more objective perspective on your thinking process.
- With a permanent written record to consult you will start to become aware of repeating themes that may point you towards core beliefs that otherwise might elude you.
- Practice makes perfect. The discipline of filling in the thought record forms is the best way to rehearse techniques

that will eventually become second nature to you. At that point you can dispense with them!

So how do they work?

Most thought records consist of a blank sheet divided into multiple columns (see Appendix 2 for an example).

Column 1: the situation

This is where you record what was going on at the time when you felt distressed. It will allow you to pinpoint relevant triggers and help you understand the context of your negative thoughts. Take note of who you were with, what you were doing and any significant changes in your environment that might be important.

Column 2: your feelings

It will almost certainly be a change in your mood that will alert you to the fact that negative thoughts are around. Record each of the emotions that you experience as specifically as you can. Try to make distinctions between different shades of feeling and be precise. Writing down that you felt *unappreciated, disappointed, lonely* and *glum* is more useful than simply putting 'felt bad' because these more accurate labels may help you access the related NATs.

In this column you also need to rate the intensity of your individual feelings, not least so that you have a baseline against which you can measure the helpfulness of your counters and alternative thoughts. You will be rerating your feelings at the end of the process. Most commonly people use percentages to do this, but you can use ratings from 1 to 10 if you prefer. There is, however, something to be said for a more differentiated scale because it allows you to track more subtle shifts. 100% would represent

> try to make distinctions between different shades of feeling and be precise

'the most intense this feeling has ever been or could possibly be' whereas 0% indicates the feeling is no longer around at all.

Column 3: your automatic thoughts

This is where you write down the NATs that come into your head at the time of the downward turn in your mood. Initially write down as many as you can. Once you have collected them you can then sort through and identify your 'hot' thoughts, i.e. the ones that seem to be the most uncomfortable or upsetting. Remember also to use the downward arrow technique to mine the underlying meaning or implication that is really doing the damage.

Column 4: The case for your negative thought or belief

In this column list the reasons why your negative thought seems believable. Pay attention to experiences that have reinforced its credibility or any arguments that appear to support it. At this stage you must allow yourself to make as strong a case for the NAT as you can – otherwise when you attempt to counter it you may not be taking on the appropriate issues.

Column 5: evidence against your negative belief

This is where you get to work using what you have learned about spotting thinking errors and the techniques described in this chapter. You need to examine the evidence in column 4 and see whether you can find any flaws in it, or the assumptions behind it. You can also marshal any further evidence at your disposal that contradicts the negative belief, paying particular attention to any personal experiences that prove the NAT may be inaccurate or biased.

Column 6: the alternative, balanced thought

In this column you will need to combine the information and arguments from the preceding two columns and see whether you can arrive at a new position that authentically takes into account all the facts and represents an objective, reasonable take on the whole matter. As mentioned before, unless it is believable it won't work, so take time to generate alternative thoughts that do justice to all the legitimate data but that are more closely aligned to your goals.

Column 7: rerate your moods

This is the moment of truth. Having worked through the process of disputing your negative thoughts and beliefs you now need to rerate the emotions you listed in column 2. Has your new, alternative thought had any impact on your mood? If the percentages have dropped – even by a little – you are on the right track. If not, you may need to re-examine the early stages of your thought record:

- Did you identify the relevant 'hot' thoughts?
- Have you been sufficiently thorough in working through the arguments 'for' and 'against'?
- Does your new, alternative thought really represent a balanced view of all the available evidence?
- Have you been consistent in the way you have rated your feelings at the start and end of the process?

Remember: CBT is all about learning new skills. The thought record is just another tool to help you in the process. If you prefer (and own a smart phone), rather than use pen and paper records you can use one of the helpful apps now available like *Thought Diary Pro, iCBT, eCBT, CBTReferee, MoodKit* or *Cognitive Diary CBT*. Several of these programs will not only help you keep accurate records of your negative thoughts and how they affected you, but will even help you identify thinking errors and prompt you to challenge them. You can find details of these apps and where to obtain them in Appendix 1. However, in whatever format you choose to record your thoughts, be aware that all the techniques in this chapter will require a little application – and not just the kind you can download to your phone. These skills take time and effort to perfect, but do persist because ultimately you will see results.

Homework: making a start with thought records

Photocopy the thought record template in Appendix 3 or make your own equivalent. Over the next two weeks try to enter some examples in the first three columns – concentrating on recording your negative thoughts, the context, and getting used to rating your different emotional response to them. Try to record five or so examples each week.

For most people it is not practical to record their thoughts at the times they experience the negative shifts, but what you do need to do is pay attention to them and try to capture them in your memory so when you do have a chance to sit down and reflect, perhaps at the end of the day or whenever you have some regular quiet time to yourself, you can record the data accurately.

The next stage is to begin disputing your thoughts using the remaining columns and aiming to generate some balanced alternatives.

Most people find they need to employ thought records for at least a couple of months before the process of disputing them becomes second nature.

CHAPTER 5

Using behaviour to change your mind

f I drop (a) a normal house brick and (b) one the same size made of paper, from a diving board, which will hit the water first? If you haven't studied physics recently, the instinctive response for most people is that the house brick, being heavier, will fall faster. In fact this is not the case. The force of gravity accelerates both objects at the same rate and, because air resistance, not mass, makes the crucial difference, both will both hit the water at much the same time. You still don't believe me? What would convince you? Maybe if you saw it with your own eyes?

According to tradition, Galileo performed just such a live demonstration by dropping a canon ball and a musket ball from the leaning tower of Pisa. Equivalent trials have been successfully repeated many times since and the findings hold. If you still need to see for yourself you can watch the Apollo 15 experiment on YouTube.

The point is that sometimes seeing really *is* believing, especially if what we are witnessing is at odds with our expectations. Knowledge gained from first-hand experience can affect us much more deeply than things we know logically must be true or that we have heard second-hand, even from the most reliable source.

Cognitive behavioural therapy recognises this, and this is why the approach makes extensive use of behavioural experiments in helping people address their negative thoughts and feelings.

Often when people complete thought records they complain that while they have satisfied themselves intellectually that their alternative thoughts are more realistic than their NATs, somehow the message doesn't get through to them in a way that makes a real difference. This is the equivalent, in popular terminology, to the difference between head knowledge and heart knowledge.

However, if a suitable experiment can be devised to test out the claims of the negative thought or substantiate the truth of the alternative new position then often the impact is greatly reinforced. Indeed when in 2003 Bennett-Levy asked a group of CBT practitioners to compare the effectiveness of keeping thought records with using behavioural experiments to challenge their negative thinking the behavioural approach won hands down.

Why is experience our best teacher?

We do not fully understand why doing something rather than reading about it or learning it from someone else affects us so powerfully, but there are several theories that shed some light on the issue.

Firstly, there is a theory that when we have a direct experience of an event we lay down multiple 'versions' of the event in our brains. These might include motor or *kinaesthetic* representations associated with our body movements, the coding of visual and auditory information about the event and physiological feedback from our bodies – sensations, emotions and so on. The idea is that the combination of all these non-verbal memory traces lodges the meaning of the experience at a deeper level. We certainly know that events that stir our emotions are much more likely to be vividly remembered.

> events that stir our emotions are much more likely to be vividly remembered

Secondly, memory and learning are also 'context-dependent'. In other words, I stand a much better chance of recalling something if I can reproduce the environment and state in which I learned it originally. One experimenter discovered that a group of students who had committed a list of facts to memory when they were drunk did a better job of recalling them when they intoxicated themselves a second time than they did when they were sober! This means that lessons learned 'in the field', i.e. based on experiments in real-life situations that deliberately trigger your depressive or anxious thoughts, are much more likely to stick when you find yourself confronted by a similar situation in future.

Adult learning theories suggest that the most natural form of learning involves a continuous cycle of learning and reflection. This certainly fits with ideas about where our negative thoughts come from in the first place. We move through the following stages when making sense of new experiences:

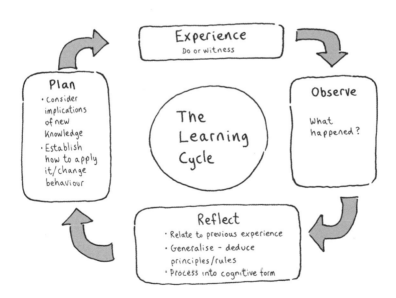

When you think about it, human infants seem to be able to learn from and generalise from their experience long before they can be formally 'taught' or reason in any conscious fashion. If experience automatically stimulates us to 'mentally digest' its lessons and incorporate them into our internal working models of the world, then action and observation may be an indispensable part of deeper learning.

Why behavioural experiments are so helpful

You will have noticed by now that a great many of our negative thoughts rely on fear-filled assumptions – assumptions about what other people are thinking or indeed what will happen to us and others if we act in certain ways. Because we anticipate the worst we tend to play it safe and avoid situations and behaviours that might confirm our worst suspicions. But, of course, if our negative thinking is unrealistic and distorts reality, then there is a good chance that many of these gloomy or anxiety-inducing predictions are false. The great benefit of behavioural experiments is that they allow us to call the bluff of our negative thoughts and test out such predictions in real-life settings. These experiments can provide us with virtually irrefutable evidence that can bring even the most entrenched false belief crashing down.

---

brilliant example

Thomas used to suffer from panicky feelings every time he travelled on the underground. As a result he stopped using the tube and has to get around London by bus or bike. He was often late as a result. Subsequently he had developed an overwhelming fear that if he had a panic attack on the underground it would escalate until he went crazy. He had a mental image of himself rampaging down the carriage, screaming uncontrollably.

Eventually, having discussed the matter with his psychologist and learning why this was unlikely to happen, he agreed to put his belief to the test by taking a trip on the Circle Line in the company of a trusted friend who agreed to get him safely off the train at the next stop if there were any signs of him losing control.

What Thomas discovered is that he did feel highly anxious during the trip, especially during the initial stages. However, he neither went crazy nor lost control. In fact he found that his anxiety, although uncomfortable, was much more bearable than he had imagined. Having been reassured that his negative beliefs were untrue, Thomas was then gradually able to build up his tolerance of tube travel to the point where he was successfully able to use the underground without undue distress.

Behavioural experiments can also be used to trial behaviour based on freshly forged alternative beliefs and see whether or not such beliefs are indeed more helpful to us. What happens if I start acting in ways more in keeping with the goals I have set for myself, maybe doing some of the things I used to enjoy before I became so depressed? What are the consequences of striking up a conversation rather than protecting myself from potential rejection by hanging back and waiting for someone to come and talk to me? These are the sorts of questions you can put to the test using behavioural initiatives.

Dropping 'safety' behaviours that make things worse

According to CBT, because of the thought–feeling–behaviour links, changing what we do as well as what we think is vital. The way we act is often a powerful maintaining factor for our problems, not least because so many of the things we do to compensate for our problems end up making them so much worse. The compensatory strategies are referred to as 'safety behaviours'.

 **example**

To understand why these safety behaviours can be so unhelpful consider the case of Rose. Rose is a 35-year-old woman who is intensely shy in social situations. Among her underlying beliefs is the conviction that 'people will think I am odd and I will be humiliated'. Usually she manages to avoid social gatherings altogether but when she can't she has attempted to compensate for her belief that people will 'see the fear in my eyes' by wearing dark classes, even indoors. Rose is also very self-conscious about her tendency to blush when she feels insecure and so has taken to wearing very thick foundation to conceal any changes in her skin tone and a silk scarf that covers her neck at all times. Whenever she cannot escape conversations with new people, Rose relies on her trusty list of 10 stock phrases that she uses to ward off embarrassing silences.

Let's consider the *intended* effects of Rose's safety behaviours and their *actual* consequences in CBT terms:

Safety behaviour	Intended effect	Actual consequence	Negative thoughts and feelings reinforced
1 Avoiding social situations	Prevents exposure to possible embarrassment	Reduces opportunities to practise social skills and build confidence No chance to collect evidence against key NATs	*'I can't cope with other people'* *'I will be humiliated'* *'Feeling embarrassed would be unbearable for me'*
2 Wearing dark glasses, heavy make-up and scarf	Conceals symptoms of self-consciousness	Draws attention to herself by making her look unusual Disrupts flow of conversation by preventing people reading her facial expressions	*'People think I am odd'* *'People find it awkward talking to me'* *'People don't want to talk to me'*

Safety behaviour	Intended effect	Actual consequence	Negative thoughts and feelings reinforced
		Scares people off by making her look aloof and reserved	*'I'm burning up with embarrassment'*
		Makes her hot and sweaty	
3 Having a set list of standard conversational gambits	Prevents mortifying silences in conversations	Makes her sound stilted and insincere	*'I come across as an oddball'*
		Prevents her from really listening to the other person	*'I feel painfully self-aware in these situations'*
		Focuses Rose on her own performance	*'I'm no good at small talk'*

What can be seen quite easily from this table is that a lot of Rose's tactics actually end up having the very opposite effect to the ones she intended. This is very often the case with safety behaviours. Paradoxically, when we take our negative thoughts at face value and act on the basis of them we usually end up strengthening them.

It is really important to become aware of your own safety behaviours because you will need to learn to abandon them if they are keeping your problems going. Make sure your temporary fixes are not stopping you from sorting out your difficulties.

exercise   Identifying your own safety behaviours

Take a moment to think about your problem and see whether you can compile a list of negative thoughts relating to it.

Looking at each thought in turn think about the ways in which it encourages you to behave. It might help to think about things that you would *stop* doing if your problem magically disappeared overnight.

Think about the potential problems that these behaviours might be making for you:

- Do they stop you from confronting your fears?
- How might they reinforce your negative beliefs?
- Do they prevent you from exposing yourself to evidence that might contradict or undermine your NATs?
- What effect do these behaviours have on other people?
- How do these behaviours leave you feeling (a) in the short term and (b) in the long term?
- In view of your understanding of the way in which thoughts, feelings and behaviours affect each other can you see any unwanted consequences of these behaviours?

My safety behaviours	Purpose or intention	Unwanted consequences
1		
2		
3		
4		

Devising behavioural experiments that work

Data gathering

There are two basic types of behavioural experiment. The first is where you put yourself in a situation to make observations and collect information. This might involve seeing whether you do actually react in the way you anticipate when you confront a scenario likely to bring your problem to the fore.

Often the most common safety behaviour of all, avoidance, means that we 'protect' ourselves from certain situations because we fear what will happen to us. Our negative thoughts tell us that exposure to the problem would be terrible for us and, of course, the more we stay away the bigger the problem becomes in our head.

brilliant tip

Remember: every time you act in a way that is consistent with your negative thoughts you are unconsciously reinforcing the notion that they must be true!

Putting yourself into a real-life situation in which you believe you are likely to have difficulties is not easy, but does give you the opportunity to get a more realistic sense of your problem and the thought processes that underpin it. It also allows you to check out whether you really need to safeguard yourself against further exposure.

The other advantage is that you will probably have much better access to the relevant NATs and emotions, because the situation will trigger them, so you will then be able to target your intervention much more effectively. This can be invaluable for people who find it hard to recall what they thought and felt after the event, and it is interesting how often people come back with a completely different set of cognitions when you send them out to monitor their thoughts directly in a real-life setting.

Finally, you may also discover that the very process of putting yourself in the anxiety-provoking situation with the explicit purpose of monitoring your thoughts and feelings and logging their intensity may give you sufficient detachment to bring your stress levels down logging their intensity may give you sufficient detachment to bring your stress levels down. Raising your self-awareness in this way keeps rational parts of your mind engaged and often stops the panic taking over.

Phone a friend?

The other form of data gathering relies on actively seeking out information and viewpoints that might help with the evaluation of negative beliefs. Someone with a phobia of flying may find it helpful to check out the actual statistics of the number of people killed in air accidents every year, or an obsessive person with irrational anxieties about catching AIDS may be reassured by researching hard facts about the ways the HIV virus is transmitted and how long it survives outside the body.

As you saw in the previous chapter, one of the most helpful counters for our biased negative thoughts is to think about the situation through the eyes of someone else, but sometimes it may be necessary to physically go and ask a sample of people for their views and perspectives. This can be particularly helpful with people prone to mind reading, who naturally tend to jump to all sorts of assumptions about what other people are thinking and feeling. Actually talking to them and finding out what they do think can expose just how far from the truth some of our more paranoid thoughts can be.

Prediction testing

The second type of experiment involves actively changing or manipulating something in order to test out the truth of a negative thought. This is the more traditional type of experiment where you check out a specific *hypothesis*, i.e. a theory about what will happen if your thought is true. If your experiment produces a result at odds with your prediction, you can be pretty sure that you need to take a long hard look at the original theory.

Turning your thoughts into predictions

Most of our negative thoughts carry implications that can be tested, but sometimes these need teasing out. If your negative thought is too vague or general it can be hard to put to the test. Experiments work best with predictions that are (a) quite specific and (b) will produce observable results. The formula to aim for is:

If X is true, then under these particular conditions Y should happen.

This does not mean that if your thought does not appear to be falsifiable through experimentation you should abandon this line of attack. What you may need to do is unpack the thought and test out some of its implications instead, thinking about what your belief would mean in practical terms across a variety of situations.

Say, for example, you held the negative belief: '*I am a terrible person*'. In its raw form this thought doesn't lend itself easily to experimental investigation. But what would 'being a terrible person' look like in practical terms? What would it mean at work? At home? In the company of friends (assuming you are not such a terrible person that you don't have any...)? What are the implications of being such a terrible person? What would a terrible person do – and what could they not do? On this basis you can start to formulate more focused predictions that you might be able to test out.

---

brilliant example

'I can't cope with life.' This is what Vanessa, a 37-year-old administrator, had been telling herself over the months she had been sinking into depression. When she started to think about experiments that might help her question this belief, Vanessa recognised she needed to look at some of her related sub-thoughts and see whether there were any specific implications of her beliefs that could be tested. She came up with the following list:

▶

Vanessa's initial NAT: '*I can't cope with life any more*'

Implications/related thoughts	Testable?	Comments
'*I have screwed up everything I care about*'	☒	Relies too much on subjective judgement
'*Past failures mean I will keep on failing*'	☑	Potentially falsifiable prediction
'*I have no reason to get out of bed any more*'	☒	Might warrant closer examination but not strictly testable
'*I have let everyone down*'	☒	Too much of a personal judgement but data-gathering survey might be useful to see if others agree
'*Even the smallest stress causes me to fall apart*'	☑	Potentially testable, providing 'falling apart' can be translated into operational terms
'*If I was at work I would make so many mistakes I would get sacked*'	☑	Could be tested but stakes are high and no opportunity to test while off sick. Might find some equivalent task and look at error rate?

Vanessa decided that the most promising of these was the implication that she would 'inevitably fail in any new challenge'. This was a much more falsifiable proposition than her initial belief but nonetheless logically related to it in her own mind. The behavioural experiment she somewhat reluctantly decided upon was to undertake a photography course and test out her hypothesis regarding the inevitability of failure.

Despite her depression, and producing a portfolio of very bleak, austere black and white photographs for her final assignment, Vanessa turned out to have quite a talent for photography. Her efforts were highly acclaimed by her tutors and even she had to admit that, by any standards, she had indeed 'succeeded' in this new venture. Becoming more active and meeting new people on the course also helped alleviate some of her depressive symptoms and the net result was that her original negative belief 'I just can't cope with life', which she had originally rated at 90%, dropped over 12 months to just 30%.

 **tip**

Decide how you are going to measure your results

When designing behavioural experiments do think carefully about how you are going to measure your results. Are there any objective benchmarks that will help you evaluate what has happened? If you rely on feelings or subjective impressions alone you may be in trouble: thinking errors such as filtering, exaggeration and polarised thinking could blunt your objectivity. Sometimes it can be helpful to recruit someone else to help you evaluate outcomes or at least develop firm criteria to which you can rate the outcome of your experiment.

Experimenting with safety behaviours

Once you have become aware of your safety behaviours, one of the most valuable experiments you can conduct is to see what happens if you drop them. The prospect of this is terrifying for most people because of the underlying belief that it is these behaviours that are protecting them from disaster.

 **example**

A conundrum

A tribe performs an elaborate rain dance every year. And every year the heavens open and it rains. Members of the tribe naturally believe that it rains because their dance has appeased the spirits. Is there another explanation? More importantly, how would you be able to prove to the chief ▶

that the dance and the rain are not necessarily connected? Can you see a connection between the tribe's attitude to the rain dance ritual and our relationship with our own safety behaviours?

Safety behaviours often allow us to create eminently testable predictions:

- 'If I don't look directly ahead and keep reciting the Lord's prayer I am bound to fall...'
- 'Unless I have a drink to relax me beforehand I will come across as awkward and tongue-tied...'
- 'If I don't make myself think about something else whenever that picture comes into my head my bad thoughts will completely take over...'
- 'Unless I wear loose, baggy clothes every day people will think I am fat...'
- 'Unless I check my body in minute detail from head to toe every day I will certainly get cancer...'

With most safety behaviours the obvious experiment is usually to take your courage in both hands and see what happens if you abandon them. Will your negative predictions come true? If this feels too threatening you can also exaggerate safety behaviours and explore the consequences of doing so. If these behaviours are so helpful to you, won't doing even more of them be even more useful? Or maybe not? Try it and see for yourself.

Challenging symptom-based predictions

These sorts of experiments can be very helpful for people who suffer from anxiety or any condition where one's own physical and psychological reactions become part of a feedback loop that make things worse.

People who suffer from panic attacks often misinterpret their own anxiety symptoms as evidence that they are on the brink of catastrophe. For example, the release of adrenaline can produce a racing heart and sensations that can be misinterpreted as signs of an impending heart attack:

> NAT: 'My racing heart means I am going to have a heart attack...'

For such people *deliberately* accelerating their heart rate, say by running up a flight of stairs a number of times, can demonstrate that a rapid pulse can be a natural and harmless reaction to increased physical demands being placed on the body such as when it prepares itself for 'fight or flight'. Unless they are predisposed to do so for some other health reason, the person concerned will *not* have a heart attack as the NAT predicts. In fact the acceleration should level off quite rapidly.

This knowledge will often help de-catastrophise the experience of a racing heartbeat the next time the person becomes anxious, and of course as they become more sanguine about the whole business a more relaxed attitude is less likely to prime a fight–flight response.

> a more relaxed attitude is less likely to prime a fight–flight response

Similar experiments can be conducted with other symptoms such as dizziness. The belief that 'feeling light-headed means I am about to lose consciousness' can be readily disproved by hyperventilating, i.e. breathing really heavily for a couple of minutes. This should bring on quite a few of the sensations experienced during a panic attack but without the feared results associated with them.

Warning: If you do decide to experiment with physical symptoms, please make sure that you take appropriate medical advice. None of these procedures will harm a healthy person but it is worth talking to your GP and making sure you are in good health before you begin.

Experimenting with assumptions underlying your NATs

Sometimes you may find it hard to think of a way to test your NAT directly, but it is worth thinking about the background assumptions on which it relies, and seeing if you can devise a way to challenge those.

brilliant example

Kay had Obsessive Compulsive Disorder (OCD). She had become terrified that if she allowed herself to mentally picture her mother in a state of ill health then somehow magically she would bring about her death. She had developed all sorts of rituals to distract her and keep this image out of her mind.

We talked about the logical impossibility of there being any significant connection between thoughts in Kay's head and her mother's physical wellbeing. However, although she acknowledged that this made sense, the risk of inviting these images into her mind just seemed too high for her.

We decided to tackle her false belief indirectly by seeing whether Kay could use her supposed mental powers to affect the health of another living creature. The underlying assumption being tested was as follows:

'What I do or don't think can influence the wellbeing of other beings.'

Kay owned a small house with a garden of which she was extremely proud. The only problem was that the cat from next door would come and defecate in her flower beds. Over the next few weeks Kay decided that she would 'will' the unsuspecting cat into an early grave. Just using the power of her thoughts she would make this happen. Each day she would say out loud five times 'Die cat, die!' and she would picture the cat becoming sicker and sicker with each passing day. Unfortunately for Kay's garden, the cat proved immune to her visualisations. Fortunately for Kay, the experiment was sufficient to introduce a chink of doubt into her conviction that her thoughts alone really could make her mother poorly.

What do I do if the results of my experiments actually end up *supporting* my negative belief?

The short answer is: don't panic! There may be many reasons why things have turned out like this:

- Check that your prediction really did target your negative thought.

- Think about what other factors might be responsible for your results.

- Did you design your experiment so that the result meant something? If you are testing the thought 'nobody wants to know me' and you get a rejection the first time you ask your friend round for coffee, that doesn't really constitute an adequate test!

- Don't give up. Remember: you can never prove something *is* true (because the exception to the rule might still be lurking out there somewhere) but you only have to prove it false once. Keep challenging your negative thoughts and see whether you can come up with alternative ways of putting them to the test. It's not easy, and it takes ingenuity and courage, but stick with it and the results will be worthwhile.

Homework: devise your own experiment

Looking at your thought records see whether you can turn your NATs and assumptions into potentially falsifiable predictions. If you are feeling brave, select one or two and see whether you can come up with an experiment to test them out.

If you are finding this difficult or too threatening, use your completed safety behaviours box on page 90 and see what happens if you deliberately abandon one of your usual strategies.

Remember: you need to work out beforehand how you are going to measure the outcome of your experiment.

CHAPTER 6

Mapping out your problems

The popcorn carton on your lap is empty and the movie is reaching its climax. The hero sits in front of the ticking bomb, watching the counter tick through the final 60 seconds. The panel having been removed, a horribly complicated skein of wires lies exposed before him. By cutting though the right wire he can deactivate the bomb and save the world from certain destruction. Sever the wrong wire and it's all over…

Strangely enough, as all devotees of the wide screen will know, despite relying almost exclusively on instinct or luck, the hero (or heroine) seldom does hack through the wrong wire. In real life, however, when it comes to disarming the mechanisms that keep our problems going we really do need to understand what is going on if we are to resolve them. In both cases what is needed, of course, is a blueprint – a useful diagram that shows how the various components are connected up and, indeed, how they affect one another.

In CBT such a blueprint is called a *formulation*. A good formulation maps out in some detail the pathways of mutual influence between the various components of the problem. It not only helps you to understand where your difficulties originated and why they are affecting you right now, but will also help you identify the thoughts, feelings and behaviours responsible for keeping the problem up and running.

Seven brilliant reasons to start formulating

Many introductory guides to CBT do not trouble the reader with advice about how to create an effective formulation but (in my view) this is a mistake. A sound formulation is an invaluable tool when tackling difficulties of all sorts:

1 It gives structure to your difficulties in a way that makes them feel more manageable.

2 Just like the wiring diagram for the bomb it can show you which connections you may need to target in order to alter or remove the problem.

3 It will help you generate theories about your problem and give you a model that can then be tested out against your experience.

4 The discipline of describing the problem in detail can help us identify key thoughts and behaviours that otherwise might be overlooked.

5 The formulation is the point at which you produce a personalised model in which the theories of CBT are made relevant to your situation and uniquely adapted to your needs.

6 A formulation can help you rate your current thinking about the problem. If your formulation doesn't hang together or make sense then that is a sure sign you may need to retrace your steps or even start from scratch.

7 A good formulation will not only help you identify the origins of your difficulties but, more crucially, help you spot the patterns of thought, feeling and action that are keeping the problem going in the present.

What's your problem?

This is a more complex question than it may at first appear because all problems can be described at a number of different levels. A woman who takes her watch to the jewellers is well

aware that she has a problem: as far
as she is concerned the problem is
that her watch is broken, she cannot
use it to tell the time and keeps running late for her appointments. In a

> all problems can be
> described at a number
> of different levels

sense it is the *effects* or consequences of the broken watch that
have become problematic for her. Just as astronomers can only
detect the existence of black holes by looking at the way they
warp the fabric of the time–space continuum around them, so
we are usually alerted to the presence of a psychological difficulty in our lives by how it affects us: either we feel bad or find
ourselves behaving in ways that we know are unhelpful for us:

- *'My nerves will stop me from giving a good speech' (and that will
  be humiliating).*
- *'I have no friends' (and that makes me feel sad and lonely).*
- *'I must go back and check I have turned the gas off even though
  I have done so 20 times already…' (and I desperately wanted to
  be on time this morning).*

When the negative outcomes of a problem alert us to its presence, we are usually quick to attach a label that appears to offer
some form of explanation. If I find myself blushing when I talk
and feel self-conscious about meeting new people I will probably conclude that my problem is 'shyness'; if I keep losing
things and forgetting to pay my bills on time I might conclude
that I am 'disorganised'.

Unfortunately these kinds of explanations actually tell us
very little about the nature of the problem. When our woman
informs the jeweller that her watch is broken, at one level she
is, of course, perfectly correct. But for the jeweller the fact
that the watch doesn't work is a description of the outcome
of a problem that he needs to redefine in terms of the watch's
component parts and the interactions between them. In order
to help the woman, her problem will need translating into the

terminology of dead batteries, over-wound springs, faulty connections, misaligned cogs and so on.

When you formulate, CBT is teaching you to think more like the jeweller. It will redirect your focus towards the mental and behavioural *processes* responsible for the negative outcomes. As we have seen, when we feel bad or act in self-destructive or irrational ways, it is usually because of what we are telling ourselves internally. You might identify your problem as a lack of confidence (outcome) but a formulation might redefine your problem as the interplay between a distorted self-image, warped thinking patterns and unhelpful patterns of behaviour (process) that feed your shyness. A good formulation will expose the inner workings of the problem and show you what thoughts and behaviours may need adjusting in order to resolve your problem's unwanted effects.

 brilliant tip

Using goals to define problems

If you are having difficulty translating your problems in CBT terms, try working backwards from the place you want to get to. Ask yourself: what will life be like once the 'problem' is resolved? What won't you be thinking/feeling/doing then? What are the specific feelings, thoughts and patterns of behaviour that currently stand in the way of achieving your objectives? If you can answer the last two questions you will usually find you are well on your way towards a useful formulation.

Pulling it all together

When you are formulating you are seeking to map out the interactions between your thoughts, feelings and behaviour. However, a comprehensive formulation will incorporate most of the following elements.

Triggers

Triggers are the events or environmental factors that kick start your train of negative thought and/or unwanted behaviour. If you can collect enough examples of your triggers you will start to become aware of common themes or repeating patterns. You will gain insight into the sense you are making of such situations and be able to target your negative thoughts and assumptions with greater accuracy.

Sue's trigger events	Common theme	Problem behaviour
1 No time to do ironing	Feeling out of control	Obsessive cleaning
2 Making a mistake on tax return		
3 Children squabbling before tea		
4 Getting drunk on night out with girls		

Ben's trigger events	Common theme	Problem behaviour
1 Argument with brother	Feeling unappreciated	Becomes needy and attention-seeking, sometimes feigning illness so he gets 'looked after'
2 Retirement party not organised for him		
3 Neighbour didn't thank him for putting out his bins		

Hot thoughts

Since distorted thinking processes are likely to be responsible for your pain it is particularly important to try to identify any negative automatic thoughts that you experienced in the vicinity of the problem.

The difficulty is that distorted thinking usually only reveals itself as such on closer examination. Most of the time we accept our negative thoughts at face value: distorted thoughts seem no less accurate or distinctive than any of the other thoughts that passed through your mind on that occasion. The relevant thoughts may not even have been conscious which, of course, makes them even harder to spot!

What you are looking for is evidence of 'hot' thoughts, which can usually be detected on the basis of the unwanted changes

what you are looking for is evidence of 'hot' thoughts

they produce – either in your mood or your behaviour. What were you thinking at that crucial moment? The questions below may help elicit the relevant negative thoughts.

Strategies for accessing hot thoughts

- *What did the trigger mean?*

  Trigger event: Examiner tells me I have failed my driving test.

  Meaning: *'I can't get anything right.'*

- *Complete the following sentence: 'When X occurred my feelings told me...'*

  Trigger event: Briefly losing child in the supermarket.

  Meaning: *'When I couldn't see Arthur my feelings immediately screamed at me that he had been taken.'*

- *What was the worst thing about [trigger event]?*

  Trigger event: Feeling unwell on the train.

  Worst implication: *'I could have fainted and been completely helpless...'*

- *If I could put the feeling into words what would they be?*

  Trigger event: Putting letter in letter box.

  Feeling in words: Guilt – 'I should have kept my mouth shut.'

- *Is there an image that more adequately summarises what I felt?*

  Trigger event: No apparent laughter in response to my joke.

  Mental image: Hostile crowd jeering and pointing at me in
                     an amphitheatre while lions run out to tear
                     me apart.

You may be aware of a whole rush of different thoughts and don't worry if you cannot initially tell which ones are the most salient. For the time being just write them all down and rate them out of a hundred in terms of how uncomfortable they make you feel. You may also find that your thoughts cluster around common themes and that there are certain NAT's that appear to summarise the tone and content of others. Finally, bear in mind that once you start trying them out in your evolving formulation the process will help clarify which thoughts are doing the real damage.

Emotions

As we have mentioned, sudden unpleasant shifts in our feelings are often the most reliable way of tracking the emergence and influence of negative automatic thoughts. Sometimes changes in our feelings may be the only trace that a NAT leaves in our consciousness. A fleeting sense of disappointment when my friend passed by and failed to acknowledge me could be the surface manifestation of a key negative thought such as: '*I am invisible… No one cares whether I am here or not.*'

When you are tracking the emotional shifts associated with an event bear in mind the following:

● Try to be aware of the whole spectrum of your feelings at the time – not just the more dominant emotions. Be specific about what you felt and at what point.

● Try to recall what you *actually* felt even if your emotions seem at odds with the situation. Don't superimpose what you assume you would have felt or should have felt in that situation. Experts on memory research point out much of what we remember is reconstructed rather than just recalled, so do your best not to use too much artistic licence.

● Be careful not to confuse the feelings that may have arisen in you *after* the problem occurred with those that may have been around at the time and that may be more closely related to the relevant NATs.

Physiological responses

An emotion is often as much a physiological event as it is a psychological one. Various hormones released by our bodies can have a profound effect on our mood. We also know that making deliberate physical changes in our outward behaviour can influence our feelings. One study found that simply by reminding themselves to smile throughout the day, subjects' reported levels of happiness were substantially increased. We also know that regular exercise can affect the body's serotonin levels in the same way as certain antidepressants. What this means is that physical sensations and changes we experience in our bodies are often important sources of information about what we are feeling and thinking.

Behaviour

This includes what you did before, during and after the trigger incident. Just as in a police statement try and be as objective, comprehensive and factual as you can. Be particularly careful of verbs that imply intentions and motives. You need to be open to the fact that actions, including your own, can easily be interpreted (and misinterpreted) in many different ways by both yourself and others.

For example, the shadowy 'drunken' stranger 'prowling around' your back garden takes on a different complexion when you discover his erratic movements and stumbling gait were the behaviours of a lost and dementing pensioner trying to find his way back to his nursing home. Never assume. Instead, try to describe the events, including your own behaviour, from a neutral third-party perspective.

Behaviour that anticipates the trigger incident can be just as revealing as your actions afterwards. Look out for safety behaviours that may have increased your vulnerability to negative cognitions. For example, if you have developed an irrational fear of strangers and therefore always take the back route away from the crowded thoroughfare, your very act of avoidance is likely to have reinforced your sense of potential danger and made you all the more jumpy when you do encounter someone.

> look out for safety behaviours that may have increased your vulnerability to negative cognitions

Predisposing factors

These are anything that has made you more vulnerable to the problem, either in the past or present. They might include key formative experiences, personality traits, unhelpful attitudes like perfectionism, or factors that may have undermined your resilience by altering your physical state like drugs, alcohol or exhaustion. The presence of certain people might make you more likely to experience your difficulties or trigger certain chains of thought. Familiarising yourself with the things that give destructive patterns more hold over you means that you can then take action either to avoid them or limit their influence.

Maintaining factors

Look out for beliefs, behaviours and any environmental factors that keep the problem going in the present. Pay particular attention to how you respond once the problem occurs and look out for unhelpful coping mechanisms and safety behaviours that are perpetuating or reinforcing negative patterns of thought, feeling and action.

Mitigating factors

It is also worth thinking about times when the problem does *not* bother you or occasions when the triggers have been present but the manifestation of your problem has been briefer or less intense. What was different? Did you react in a different way? Did someone else help you to stay calm and, if so, what did they do that helped? Was the impact of the trigger offset by other positive experiences that day?

Thinking about mitigating factors can give you important clues about how best to tackle your problems. If you can work out what helped and why, you can do more of it, weaken the cycle and start to protect yourself.

Three key principles for winning formulations

Principle 1: keep thinking about how things connect up

When you are formulating, remember that just like the jeweller you need to think of your problem as a system of interrelated parts. In this case the main components are elements of your thoughts, feelings and behaviour. You have to be aware not only of which parts in the system you need to focus on, but also how they affect each other. How useful your formulation will be to you depends on how accurately you are able to trace out the critical pathways of cause and effect.

You will remember from Chapter 2 that we talked about the 'two-way street' principle – for example that thoughts can influence emotions and that the same emotions can prime or reinforce certain thoughts? When you are formulating half the trick is to keep your eyes open for these kinds of feedback loops, because it is these that make a problem become entrenched.

Principle 2: narrow the focus

Sometimes people can feel that they have so many different problems or that they are so involved that they don't know where to start. The prospect of trying to get it all down on paper seems daunting. The solution is simple: don't. One of the joys of CBT is that it allows you to break complex problems down into smaller, more manageable chunks. Looking in detail at a specific example of just one way in which your difficulties are affecting you is often the most reliable way to access key cognitions and behaviours that have a wider relevance. Understanding how you reacted in one situation in which a problem revealed itself will usually give you insight into others. For example, you may spot a tendency towards a particular thinking error that you also make in other contexts.

brilliant tip

Think like a detective

The nature of problems is to feel muddled and overwhelming but in order to describe the problem adequately for CBT purposes you will need to identify the thoughts, feelings and behaviours associated with your problem in specific, concrete terms. This is why it can be helpful to concentrate on a particular incident and go over it in fine

▶

detail. The process is not far removed from the forensic investigation of a crime scene. You know something untoward has obviously taken place – in this case what George Orwell described as a 'thought crime' – but in order to work out what has happened and who is responsible the crime scene needs to be scrutinised and the traces of evidence rigorously collated, catalogued and examined.

CBT regards our day-to-day difficulties as manifestations of deeply rooted habits and processes that operate in much the same way across different contexts, so the chances are that any significant example of the problem is likely to tap into the relevant underlying patterns of thought and behaviour.

Remember, you don't have to formulate every aspect of your difficulties right away. Mapping out just one aspect of your problems in a way that suggests strategies for controlling a particular symptom is helpful and may well be the best place to start. Understanding one domain or subsystem of the total problem is likely to provide insights into connections with other aspects of your difficulties.

Principle 3: treat your formulation as a work in progress

In CBT the formulation is never the finished product or a definitive account of the problem. In keeping with the exploratory spirit of the whole CBT approach your formulation is always provisional so along the way expect to redraw it, add new bits to it and lose others. This is entirely to be expected: it does not mean you have 'got it wrong', it is part of the process of making sense of your difficulties. As Thomas Edison, the great American inventor, once pointed out: 'Just because something doesn't do what you planned doesn't mean it's useless.'

> your formulation is always provisional so along the way expect to redraw it

Just as the early cartographers had to redraw their maps as they developed better instruments, so be ready to make changes. A formulation is just a starting point, a set of hypotheses about your problem that may need to be updated as you learn more about it.

Indeed one of the functions of a formulation is to translate your problem into a set of testable theories. As you conduct experiments or adapt your behaviour on the basis of your formulation, you will be putting those theories to the test. Depending on your results you may need to revise your formulation, or even go back to the drawing board and start again. This is a natural and helpful part of the process in which theory is constantly revised in the light of new experience.

 **brilliant** tip

'Can you see what it is yet...?'

The usual (but not only) way to represent a formulation is in the form of a diagram consisting of boxes joined up with many arrows. There are several advantages of employing this method.

Firstly, it is much easier to think about the relationships that exist between the different elements. You might, for example, depict a causal connection between a belief (e.g. 'Trying to deal with my problems is pointless') and aspects of your behaviour (e.g. procrastinating and watching daytime TV).

However, seeing a diagram laid out in front of you may also trigger the realisation that this pattern of behaviour is linked into other negative thoughts such as 'I can't get my act together' which in turn is linked to emotions (such as embarrassment) that encourage you to watch more daytime TV so you don't have to expose yourself to the judgement of other people. You have discovered a feedback loop!

▶

Isolating the different elements in a visual form will encourage you to consider links and pathways between them that may have escaped your attention. You can also easily try out different permutations and combinations by shuffling the elements and connections around until you develop a network that makes adequate sense of your problem.

Finally, because the web of connections and associations mirrors the way the brain naturally encodes information, mapping out the system in this way is also likely to cue the recall of new relevant information or facets of the problem that might have been overlooked. Tony Buzan (author and educational consultant) claims that this is one of the advantages of mind mapping, which is based on almost identical principles.

 **brilliant** example

Peter's short fuse

To illustrate the process involved in arriving at an adequate formulation we shall use the example of Peter, a 25-year-old banker. Peter was round at his girlfriend's last Friday. The evening had been going well, but when they got back to Peter's flat they had a blazing row. The girlfriend left in tears and Peter downed a bottle of scotch before collapsing unconscious on the sofa. The next day the girlfriend texts Peter and informs him that the relationship is over.

Peter knows he has a problem. Try as he might he seems unable to hold down a long-term relationship. His love life is a catalogue of failed romances and unsatisfying one-night stands. Bizarrely, all his relationships end in much the same way. At the moment Peter doesn't really understand what is going wrong. He decides the time has come to enlist the help of some CBT principles to try to find out.

'Where did it all go wrong?' Searching for the emotional shift

In order to isolate the relevant thoughts, feelings and behaviours, Peter knew he needed to pinpoint the moment the problem began to manifest itself. Peter believed the evening had been going well up to the argument with Laurie. But what were they arguing about? What kicked off the conflict between them? One moment they were fine, the next they were at each other's throats. What had changed?

Peter mentally replayed the events of the night before, this time focusing on the way his feelings altered over the course of the evening. He recalled being excited and happy on his way to meet Laurie at the station and pleased when he saw her walking towards him. In the restaurant he had felt relaxed and confident in her company, but when they got through the door of the flat something she said turned off all those positive feelings almost as if she had flicked a switch.

After that a wave of very different emotions had swept over him: he felt angry and hurt and, as he pictures them sitting there on the sofa, he could also detect echoes of two other emotions – shame and embarrassment. Suddenly, Peter found he could recollect with great clarity what Laurie said that upset him so much: 'Maybe next time we could try that Indian in the high street?'

 **tip**

Fire up your memory

Peter had a conveniently recent example of his problem to draw upon but this is not always the case. However, this does not mean that all is lost.

In order to analyse your own behaviour and reactions you will need to bring the triggering event to mind as vividly as possible. Try to recall as much detail about the situation as possible – even if it

▶

seems irrelevant. Because of the way our memory works, traces of an event are all connected and recalling one aspect of an event can often trigger other memories. Sensory information is often evocative: can you remember distinctive smells, tastes, textures associated with the target event? What were you wearing? Do you recall what you were doing before the incident took place? Setting the event in context by thinking about other events that took place around the same time can often trigger recall.

Sometimes, to give yourself access to the thoughts and feelings associated with an event, it can even be helpful to physically revisit the scene where it took place. A client of mine who had been involved in a bad road traffic accident could not, try as he might, access any of the NATs associated with the accident itself, even though he had been unable to travel by car since. Only when he visited the scene of the accident was he able to recall exactly what he had thought and felt in the moments before the collision. He was then able to begin tackling the distorted thoughts that had prevented him from getting back behind the wheel.

Identifying the hot thoughts

To you and I, Laurie's comment about trying the Indian restaurant may seem like a fairly innocuous suggestion, but for Peter it had unleashed a flood of negative automatic thoughts. Becoming aware of this, Peter's next task in developing his formulation was to specify the content of those thoughts.

to isolate the NATs responsible for negative feelings dig a little deeper

Allowing himself to focus on Laurie's remark and re-experience the emotions that he felt, Peter found it not too difficult to recall the conclusion that this remark had prompted: 'She obviously didn't like the meal tonight…' However, Peter recognised that this thought didn't explain the strength of his reactions. In order to isolate the NATs responsible for his negative feelings he had to dig a little deeper. He used the downward arrow technique and the questions outlined earlier in this chapter to begin eliciting his NATs.

Using these lines of questioning Peter's first attempt to identify the relevant NATs produced the following ladder of implications. The 'hot thought', i.e. the one that produced the strongest surge of emotion and seemed to sum up the other thoughts he identified was, 'I am a failure.'

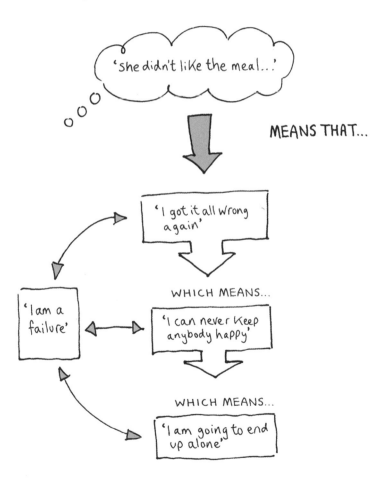

Peter now had a potential candidate for the thought responsible for his feelings and behaviour the previous night. He was in a position to begin completing a basic CBT template.

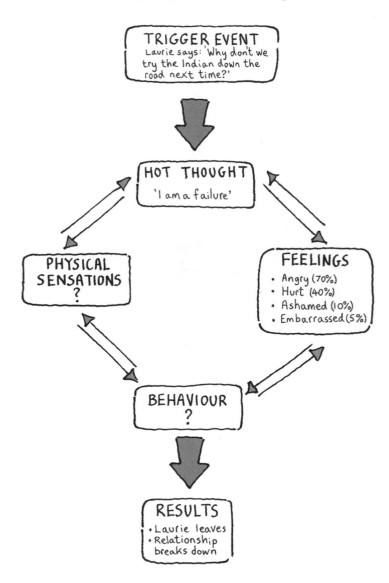

However, looking at the links between the thought and the emotions in Peter's chart it becomes clear that something is amiss. While he recognised that his identified hot thought 'I am a failure' might generate feelings of shame and embarrassment, emotions like anger and hurt did not tally so readily with the target thought. This tension became even more exaggerated once Peter began to examine evidence to complete the boxes relating to *physical sensations* and *behaviour*.

Peter was already aware that the couple had argued, but looking more objectively at his behaviour he could see that he had responded quite aggressively to Laurie's suggestion. His *actions* had included:

- raising his voice
- initially glaring at her without blinking or breaking eye contact
- announcing that he wasn't sure he wanted to go out with her again anyway
- making several critical remarks about Laurie's behaviour the day before
- turning his back on her once the argument became heated and heading for the kitchen
- smashing several glass bottles into the recycling box.

He was also able to recall several *physiological changes* that had taken place at the same time:

- His heart rate had accelerated.
- He recalled a horrible knotted feeling in the pit of his stomach.
- He had felt 'light-headed' and was aware he was breathing quite heavily.
- He could remember clenching his fists and them feeling quite hot and sweaty when he did so.

Revising your formulation in the light of new evidence

We have already noted that there appeared to be only a partial correspondence between what Peter felt in response to the trigger and the emotions he experienced immediately afterwards. This is not to say that the thought processes Peter had uncovered were invalid or irrelevant, but his activated core belief 'I am a failure' did not fully account for either his behaviour or subsequent physiological response on this occasion.

The thought he had uncovered is more typically connected with more passive, depressive patterns that usually encourage the person to withdraw into himself. Peter's response was very different. He had initially come out 'all guns blazing', so having fed this new information into the diagram Peter realised it was time to scrutinise the incident for another possible NAT that might better account for his overreaction.

Having tested the formulation out against the model Peter now has to go back to the drawing board and see whether Laurie's reaction could have had another meaning for him that might better explain his reaction. Opposite is his second attempt.

Feeding this new 'hot' thought ('I am under attack!') instantly made much more sense of his feelings and subsequent behaviour. Jumping to the conclusion that Laurie was criticising him, Peter had felt wounded and then reacted by striking back. The anger that rushed through him was part of a natural defensive reaction as his body prepared itself for combat. Peter also realised that this new account was much more consistent with the physical sensations he had experienced as the adrenaline had set his pulse racing.

What was becoming clear to Peter as he reflected upon the events of the night before was that he has a problem with anger, and that his hypersensitivity to criticism was costing him his love life.

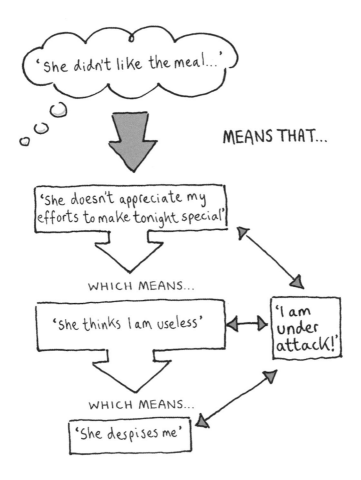

Looking at the emerging formulation and the interactions between the different areas of the diagram, Peter realised there were various ways in which he could learn to protect himself from the consequences of his anger.

Possible interventions

- He could stop interpreting everything other people said to him as a personal attack and challenge his NATs with balanced alternative thoughts.

- He could practise relaxation techniques such as diaphragmatic breathing or visualisation to calm his body's fight–flight reactions.

- He could learn to modify his actions, lower his tone and make his body language less threatening.

- He could express his feelings with greater clarity at the time and resolve potential misunderstandings rather than avoiding his anger and letting it build towards an explosion.

Because of the way thoughts, feelings and behaviours are all connected, any of these interventions would probably have helped. A combination of all of them might have averted Peter's romantic suicide altogether. The joy of a good formulation is that it opens up various options for tackling your problems and a multi-pronged approach is often precisely what is required.

the joy of a good formulation is that it opens up various options

Elaborating the formulation

Of course beginning to understand the events of that one night was only the start for Peter. Reflecting on parallels with other incidents in his life, Peter began to flesh out his formulation.

He looked at predisposing factors that included the constant stream of criticism he had been exposed to as a child, and began to see that the cocky, arrogant air he assumed at work was actually a compensatory strategy to mask his damaged self-esteem.

The emerging formulation also showed him how fear of further humiliation had prompted Peter to develop a number of 'protective' assumptions and safety behaviours that guaranteed yet more heartache and rejection and were reinforcing his beliefs that he was unlovable and inadequate.

As he reviewed his thought records over the next few weeks Peter also became more aware of the thinking errors and distortions he mobilised to keep his set of dysfunctional assumptions and negative beliefs in place. He learnt to appreciate how polarised thinking, emotive language and rampant catastrophising was closing down opportunities for the intimacy he longed for. A simplified version of Peter's more elaborate formulation is shown overleaf.

Over the next seven months Peter used his formulation to make a plan of campaign. He learnt relaxation techniques to bring his state of anxious arousal under control. He conducted experiments that involved breaking some of his own taboos. He sought to find alternative interpretations of the behaviour of people around him. He cut back on the drinking and other safety behaviours that were compounding his problems.

Over time colleagues gradually noticed the changes in Peter, and the general consensus was that he had become a more approachable, less pushy individual. Despite this, Peter felt he had more work to do on the legacy of his childhood before he would be ready for a serious relationship. For the time being he decided to concentrate on developing his friendships. However, he was also in no doubt that the process of mapping out his problems in an objective and analytical way had been the start of a personal revolution. At our last session he spoke optimistically about the future: 'I don't know whether I will get the girl or not...' he mused, 'but hopefully I won't be acting like a total jerk when she does come looking for me...'

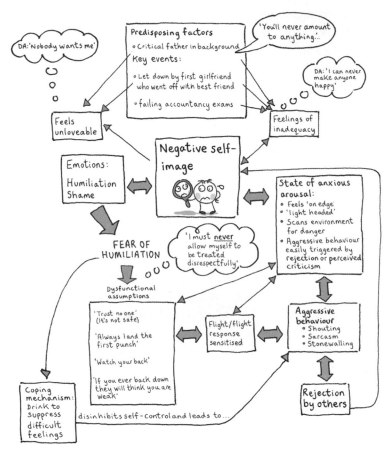

Peter's emerging formulation

Homework: make a start on your own formulation

Set aside some time this week to begin working on a formulation of
your own problems.

Start by analysing one example of your problem in detail and then
see whether you can detect themes that apply in other areas of
your life.

Don't feel you have got it right first time. Remember formulating is a process and often one of trial and error at that. However, do try to devise at least one behavioural experiment that will allow you to confirm whether or not you are working along the right lines.

CHAPTER 7

Beating the blues

'You largely constructed your depression. It wasn't given to you. Therefore, you can deconstruct it.'

Albert Ellis, American psychologist and psychotherapist

At any given time, conservative estimates state that between 15% and 20% of the adult population are suffering from significant depressive symptoms. Because depression has become so commonplace we can easily underestimate the misery it causes. The real tragedy is that so much of this distress is unnecessary. CBT offers a tried and tested model of depression and treatment strategies that have good rates of success when diligently applied.

You may remember from Chapter 1 that Beck pioneered CBT as a treatment for depression back in the sixties. His original formulation of depression and the techniques he devised for tackling it have scarcely been modified since then, although recently combining CBT with practices borrowed from the Eastern meditation practice known as *mindfulness* are producing promising results, especially when it comes to preventing relapse.

Are you depressed?

We all feel down from time to time, but to establish whether you might be suffering from clinical depression have a look at the following checklist:

☐ Do you feel consistently low most days?

☐ Do you find it hard to motivate yourself and take pleasure in things?

☐ Have you lost or gained significant amounts of weight recently? (People who are depressed either lose their appetite or tend to comfort eat.)

☐ Are you sleeping much more or less than usual?

☐ Do you feel restless, jittery and unable to settle much of the time or find yourself feeling unusually sluggish and listless?

☐ Do you feel tired and drained most days?

☐ Do you feel especially worthless or guilty?

☐ Are you finding it hard to concentrate and remember things at the moment?

☐ Do you have recurrent thoughts about dying (even if you have no intention of acting on them)?

If you answered yes to five or more of these questions and your symptoms have persisted for at least two weeks then the chances are you may be suffering from a major depressive episode.

Depression is a serious illness. It currently accounts for 75% of all admissions to psychiatric wards and severe depression can even be accompanied by psychotic episodes when people lose touch with reality and may experience delusions or hallucinations. While obviously only a tiny minority of cases become anywhere near this extreme, these statistics do emphasise that depression should not simply be ignored.

statistics emphasise that depression should not simply be ignored

The longer depression is left untreated the harder it becomes to deal with. If you think you are suffering from clinical depression don't suffer in silence. Hopefully, the techniques described in this chapter will be of help to you, but do talk to your GP if you feel your symptoms are not shifting; your GP will be able to refer you to a suitable therapist.

It is worth noting that there are various forms of depression. People who suffer from *bipolar depression* typically find that they alternate between crashing lows and periods when they are filled with manic energy. At such times people tend to feel great but often find themselves acting in impulsive or irresponsible ways – wild spending sprees and indiscrete sexual behaviour are not uncommon during manic phases. However (perhaps unfairly) not everyone who suffers from a bipolar disorder experiences the manic highs but may still require specialist treatment.

If you think you are depressed it is worth talking to your doctor who can advise you regarding appropriate investigations and treatment options.

A word about drugs

You do not have to choose between taking prescribed antidepressants and using cognitive behavioural techniques. Trials by the National Institute of Clinical Excellence established that for most people a combination of CBT and antidepressants is often the most effective treatment. In practice some people find that with antidepressants taking the edge off their organic depressive symptoms they can actually make better use of CBT techniques.

Obviously the decision to take any kind of medication is a personal call, but some individuals put themselves under enormous unnecessary pressure in relation to this issue. Remember you can always try medication and if, on balance, you find it helps you then all well and good. However, if the side effects start outweighing the benefits you can always go back to your GP to consider alternative ways forward. If you have doubts about the merits of medication, talk them through with your doctor. This commits you to nothing but will equip you to make a more informed choice.

 **example**

Duncan was the youngest in his family. His birth was not planned and his parents were both a bit shell-shocked when his mother fell pregnant at the age of 46. They weren't prepared to have to revisit nappies and sleepless nights, especially since his eldest brother had just set off for university and they were looking forward to having time to pursue their own interests.

Unfortunately their resentment had communicated itself to Duncan. Deep down he felt unwanted and an inconvenience to his family. ('There was always this slight sense of three's a crowd...') Nevertheless, Duncan was a bright and popular child and did well at school. His childhood was generally unremarkable and, despite sometimes appearing rather driven, he appeared a happy, well-adjusted boy.

Duncan met Jennifer at college and they married shortly after they graduated. He got a sought-after post in a prestigious marketing company. Everything seemed to be going well for the young couple, and one day when he returned from work Jennifer announced that she was expecting a baby.

Both parents were delighted, but shortly after the birth of their daughter, Molly, Duncan noticed that his mood was changing. He felt fed up and became uncharacteristically snappy. Jennifer was constantly busy with Molly and, although he loved his daughter, Duncan found himself feeling increasingly resentful of how little time they had together. 'I just feel a bit shut out,' he complained. Friends told him this was entirely normal in the early months and Duncan dismissed his low mood as a function of disrupted sleep and adjusting to the upheaval of a new baby.

However, as the weeks went by, things got worse. Duncan became more and more withdrawn. He found it hard to concentrate at work and at weekends he could hardly drag himself out of bed – which inevitably became a real issue for Jennifer who understandably felt she wanted some help with Molly having looked after her all week.

The family struggled on, but over the next few months a downturn in the economy started to make Duncan's position at work look increasingly vulnerable. During a recent performance review his boss had expressed concern about their declining sales figures and Duncan became obsessed with fears about being made redundant, even though there were no indications that this was likely. 'I know I am not coping with anything any more,' he told me. 'It can only be a matter of time before they realise what a liability I am and chuck me out. Then what's going to happen to us? It doesn't bear thinking about. Maybe it would be better for everyone if I just didn't exist...' Looking haggard and tearful as he said this, all the evidence pointed to the fact that Duncan was now in the grip of a major depressive episode.

Beck's model of depression

Beck proposed that some people are often vulnerable to depression because of negative assumptions laid down in childhood. Under normal circumstances, he suggested, these beliefs may lie dormant but a critical incident is all it takes to activate them and unleash a stream of associated negative thoughts. Repeated exposure to these thoughts, Beck argued, in due course produces the organic, physical symptoms of a depressive disorder.

> a critical incident is all it takes to unleash a stream of associated negative thoughts

In Duncan's case, his parents' reaction to having an unplanned child had contributed to assumptions and core beliefs about being unwanted and unvalued. These niggling misgivings had not troubled him unduly during his upbringing, offset as they were by many other positive experiences. He had felt secure in his peer group and felt that his good grades at school gave him tangible proof of his worth, especially since his marks had also

Worked example of Beck's model of depression

earned him the approval of his parents. When Duncan met Jennifer, the intimacy between them gave him a real sense of belonging that largely buried the insecurities of his childhood and his success at work continued to build his self-esteem.

For Duncan the birth of Molly proved the critical incident that activated his childhood assumptions. Jennifer's preoccupation with the baby triggered Duncan's old fears of exclusion. He felt that now she had Molly, Jennifer no longer wanted or needed him. Suddenly all his negative core beliefs were up and running, producing a steady stream of unhelpful NATs that were soon dragging Duncan into a spiral of depression.

As the depression took hold, Duncan's unhelpful core beliefs started to become self-fulfilling prophecies: his irritability and passivity at home did start to distance him from his wife while concentration difficulties and low levels of motivation laid him open to criticism at work. Since his self-esteem was so closely tied into his perceived success, the loss of his status as a rising star within the company hit him hard and made him even more susceptible to the impact of his buried core beliefs. His fears that he would ultimately be rejected professionally, as well as personally, flowed naturally from his underlying convictions: 'I am not really wanted' and 'Other people are more valuable than me'.

How depressed people think

We normally think of depression as synonymous with low mood but, having read this book it will come as no surprise to learn that depression is a condition that affects how we think and behave. The poet Sylvia Plath described depression as like looking at the world through a bell jar – an image that emphasises just how distorted the thinking of a depressed person can become.

Beck noted that the thoughts of depressed people tend to reflect the following themes:

1 **Critical thoughts about the self**
   - 'I'm stupid.'
   - 'I've stuffed up again.'
   - 'No one could care about me.'
   - 'I am bad through and through.'

2 **A bleak, negative view of other people and the world in general**
   - 'People always let you down.'
   - 'The world is a vicious place.'
   - 'Everyone's out for themselves.'

3 **A pessimistic outlook on the future**
   - 'Nothing good lasts for long.'
   - 'There's no point trying – I will only fail.'

Maintaining factors in depression

In order to maintain these depressive assumptions, depressed people tend to use a broad repertoire of characteristic cognitive distortions including *polarised thinking*, *filtering*, *personalisation* and *generalisation* (see Chapter 3 for details).

When explaining negative events depressed people tend to hold themselves responsible – even when they are not necessarily to blame. Any mistakes they do make are magnified and taken as examples of engrained character flaws rather than a function of particular circumstances. Needless to say they see little hope that the situation will improve.

As in Duncan's case the *behaviour* of depressed people only tends to reinforce the cycle of negative thinking. Because depressed people tend to become withdrawn and lethargic, they often make themselves feel worse. By behaving in this way they no longer provide themselves with experiences and opportunities that might challenge their sense of helplessness and worthlessness.

Moreover their passivity provides ample opportunity for depressed people to reflect on their shortcomings and reinforce their pessimistic thinking style. *Compulsive rumination* – endlessly going over the same problem-saturated scenarios – is a key characteristic of such individuals.

Taking things easy when you feel this fragile seems at face value like a sensible thing to do, but as they withdraw from everyday routines depressed people unwittingly confirm how badly they are coping with life. As a brilliant student of CBT, you will already have recognised that this is actually a classic safety behaviour, and like most safety behaviours it spells trouble.

> depressed people unwittingly confirm how badly they are coping with life

Cognitive strategies for tackling depression

Cognitive behavioural treatments for depression usually involve a multi-pronged attack on the various maintaining factors we have just described. In the later stages of treatment, you may also find it helpful to target the core beliefs and assumptions that may have made you vulnerable to depression in the first place.

There are four main cognitive techniques for addressing depressed thinking styles:

1 decentring yourself from your depressive thoughts
2 distraction techniques to halt unhelpful rumination
3 challenging cognitive distortions using thought records
4 activating problem-solving skills to counteract feelings of helplessness.

1 Decentring yourself from your depressive thoughts

It all sounds a bit Californian, doesn't it? What decentring actually involves is learning to step back from your depressive thoughts and observe them rather than being so immersed that you can no longer separate yourself from them.

When you are closely identified with your depressive thoughts it is almost impossible to do anything about them. When you become conscious of your depressive thoughts and feelings for what they are, i.e. just patterns of thoughts and feelings intruding into your awareness, you automatically weaken their power.

Decentring is the essence of the 'mindfulness' approach. Rather than trying to grapple with your thoughts, the mindfulness tradition encourages you simply to observe the flow of your consciousness while adopting an accepting, non-judgemental stance. Instead of trying to control your depressive thoughts directly you notice them, label them and allow them to pass through your mind unobstructed. This is in stark contrast with the nature of depressive rumination which usually involves mentally grabbing on to a misery-inducing scenario and making it play in your head over and over again.

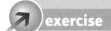 **exercise**   Living in the moment: the 'eat-a-peach' challenge

An exercise conducted in the first session of many mindfulness groups involves nothing more complicated than eating a piece of fruit while concentrating fully on the experience and how it affects you. The rationale is that we spend much of our lives in a state of divided attention. A bit like a computer with several programs up and running at the same time we are quite capable of automatically running depressive processing subroutines alongside whatever else we are doing.

By learning to live fully 'in the moment' and gently bringing awareness back to bear on incoming sensory information (the feel of the peach in your hand, the levels of muscular tension in your body, the feeling of the warm evening breeze on your skin) the goal is to channel your awareness into a single integrated channel that diverts energy away from fruitless rumination – no pun intended.

This may strike you as deceptively easy but just try it! Mindfulness belongs to a meditative tradition long established in the east, and like all meditation practices it is a discipline that requires considerable practice to perfect. My advice is that if this approach appeals to you, then follow the link http://mbct.co.uk/the-mbct-programme and contact a local group where you can practise with the support of others and quite possibly the guidance of a suitable psychologist.

2 Distraction techniques

These involve using more active strategies to interrupt the flow of negative thinking. You can use the same kinds of *sensory awareness* techniques described above to anchor yourself in your surroundings. Describing in detail what you can see around you, the sounds you can hear and even tactile sensations can shift your focus away from your thoughts. Some people find that pinging an elastic band worn on the wrist whenever a depressive thought enters their head can also provide a brief, alternative, sensate focus as well as training them to become more aware of bad cognitive habits.

Alternatively you can try setting yourself a *distracting mental task*. Count back from a hundred in threes or try setting anagrams in your head. Tongue twisters can also provide a handy and demanding activity that will monopolise your concentration and temporarily stop depressive rumination in its tracks.

3 Challenging cognitive distortions

This involves using the skills described in Chapter 4 to counter the content of your negative thoughts and beliefs. Below is a sample thought record from Tracy, a retired nurse suffering from depression, illustrating how these techniques can be used to work towards more balanced thoughts to use as an antidote to depressive NATs.

Trigger	Watching people go to work from the window
Emotions	Feel bleak 80%
	Resigned 60%
	Hollow feeling in pit of stomach 50%
NATs	'I am no use to anyone'
	'I am a drain and a burden' (85%)
	'I'm all washed up'

Evidence supporting negative thought:

- I am not working any more.
- My children are all grown up and don't need me.
- My hospital appointments for my rheumatism take up time and money that would be better spent on someone younger.

Evidence challenging negative thought:

- My friends seem to enjoy my company.
- Without me as bridge partner, Margaret wouldn't leave the house day in day out.
- My value doesn't depend on what I do but who I am.
- My children may not need me physically, but Sarah still uses me as a shoulder to cry on when the twins are getting too much for her.
- I am an active and involved grandmother.
- When I was a nurse I believed that the good thing about the NHS was that it was available to everyone – there's no reason that shouldn't include me.

Alternative thought/more balanced position:
'Just because I am not working doesn't mean my life has no value or that I am not making a valid contribution to other people' (85%).

4 Problem-solving approaches

Feeling helpless and disenfranchised is one of the characteristic feelings of depressed people. They can feel that they have no resources to tackle problems in their own lives or those of anyone else. Consciously using problem-solving strategies can make even depressed individuals feel more empowered. For example, if your negative thoughts are telling you that the world is a bleak uncaring place, try brainstorming things you personally could do to make a difference – perhaps volunteering for a charity or even just writing a letter to a friend. There are often constructive ways forward even with personal situations that feel hopeless, despite what your depression would tell you. Try to identify three things you could do that would improve your situation, however slightly. If you are struggling to do this, why not

> using problem-solving strategies can make even depressed individuals feel more empowered

enlist the help of a practically minded friend or relative who could help you come up with some ideas?

Behavioural strategies for tackling depression

Behavioural approaches are indispensable when tackling depression. One study found that people who used the behavioural techniques described below reported higher rates of symptom relief than those who exclusively used a cognitive approach. Obviously this is a bit of a false distinction since, as you have learned, behavioural interventions do directly impact on our thoughts and feelings. However, the point is that when it comes to sorting out depression, what you do is just as important, if not *more* important, than mental strategies alone. Behavioural techniques include:

1 activity scheduling
2 behavioural experiments to challenge depressive assumptions
3 exercise.

1 Activity scheduling

This is one of the simplest interventions but also one of the most effective for depressed people. We have already illustrated how passivity and withdrawal are the two most typical safety behaviours practised by depressed individuals. Low energy levels, reduced motivation and exaggerated fears that they will make pretty poor company encourage such individuals to 'hole up' and do less and less. Often severely depressed people find it hard to do much more than lie in bed all day. Unfortunately, for reasons discussed above, giving in to the temptation of retreating and closing down is a policy that makes depressive symptoms worse.

Activity scheduling is a tool for combating passivity and gradually re-engaging the depressed person in some of the routines of his or her everyday life. At the same time it allows you to test out predictions based on depressive assumptions ('I don't enjoy anything these days...'; 'I'm just a useless waste of space...').

The first step in activity scheduling is simply to monitor one's activity over a week by recording on a grid like the one below how you spend every hour. A brief entry is fine, but at the end of the hour make sure you also rate from 0 to 100 how bad your symptoms have been, i.e. how depressed you have felt during that hour. The benefits of doing this are twofold:

1 It allows you to take a baseline reading of your current activity levels. Often this can be a pleasant surprise in itself since many depressed people feel they achieve 'absolutely nothing'

during the day (polarised thinking). Realising that they may have already been doing more than they think can start to break the cycle of paralysis. If activity levels have been severely restricted, at least you will be in a position to set realistic goals for yourself during the next phase.

2 By rating symptom intensity alongside your activities you will be able to work out the circumstances that make you feel more depressed and identify activities that take the edge off your symptoms. By analysing these patterns you can gradually introduce more of those activities that help you.

This is all very simple, obvious stuff but it introduces a level of objectivity and structure that you can very easily lose when the 'black dog' of depression threatens to take control.

Example of activity monitoring grid

Time	MONDAY		TUESDAY	
	Activity	Symptom intensity	Activity	Symptom intensity
8.00–9.00	Lay in bed going over things.	90%	Had to get up to take Cassie to station first thing. Showered. Ate piece of toast.	70%
9.00–10.00	Took dog for walk.	70%	Took dog out.	65%
10.00–11.00	Mick called round for coffee. Couldn't concentrate on conversation.	85%	Helped with stocktaking at Oxfam shop.	50%
11.00–12.00	Went back to bed.	80%	More stocktaking. Felt too exhausted to continue.	60%
12.00–etc.				

The next step

After you have done a week of recording, now is the time to use your knowledge to start pushing your activity levels up a little at a time. The key to doing this is to set realistic goals for yourself.

Rating how much you enjoy each of your planned activities (Pleasure rating: 0–100) and the sense of achievement it gives you (Mastery: 0–100) immediately afterwards will also help you confound your depressive expectations and start to help you feel less powerless. You can also use this information to schedule future activities likely to boost your mood.

brilliant tip

The nature of depression is to feel overwhelmed. It is therefore really important not to be too ambitious in the targets that you set yourself – particularly in the early stages – and to make your goals very concrete and specific. If you bite off more than you can chew you will simply compound a sense of failure and strengthen the very thoughts and beliefs you are trying to weaken.

When you do start small be aware that your depression will tell you that what you are attempting is so modest that it won't make any difference: 'What does it matter if I get up at a regular time everyday? Big deal...' However, as you master small, localised goals you will begin to build confidence for more ambitious projects. The whole process will gather momentum. As a famous oriental proverb states: 'The journey of a thousand miles begins with a single step...' Don't let your depressive 'all-or-nothing-thinking' blind you to the truth of this.

 **brilliant** example

Alex Johnson was a retired pilot who had become severely depressed following the death of his wife. Previously sociable and outgoing, Alex had become a virtual recluse, sitting at home and watching sport on the television day in, day out. This gave him ample opportunity to mull over how old and helpless he had become. As he cut himself off from his friends at the local rotary club Alex also lost confidence in his social skills. He kept telling himself that he was not 'fit company' at the moment and it would be far better if he waited until he was less depressed before he made any social overtures.

It was not easy to convince Alex that he was unlikely to feel better *until* he resumed the social activities that previously played such an important role in his life. His negative thoughts had convinced him that he was bound to embarrass himself and that everyone would notice how changed he was (catastrophising). In any case there seemed little point because, Alex insisted, he knew he would not enjoy himself.

In therapy Alex examined and started to consider the distorted assumptions that were keeping him secluded. How realistic were his fears? How obvious would the outward signs of his depression be to others?

After much gentle persuasion and some controlled 'dry runs' in the form of meals out with family members, Alex finally agreed to cross the threshold of his local club. He sensibly arranged for one of his friends to collect him and we agreed that he would stay for a minimum of half an hour.

In the event the other club members were delighted to see him, and Alex coped better than expected. He admitted that although he had been more subdued than usual he had nevertheless been 'on surprisingly good form'. Certainly the anticipated public humiliation did not occur, and Alex confessed that 'it had been good to see some familiar faces'.

Alex's courage paid dividends. Building on this experience, over the next few months Alex started picking up the threads of his social life and frequented the club on a regular basis. The subsequent change in his demeanour and the accompanying reduction in his depressive symptoms were striking.

2 Using behavioural experiments to challenge depressive assumptions

Depressive assumptions and beliefs can usually be translated into testable predictions. This is well worth doing, even though your depressed mind might be telling you there is little to be gained and these kinds of experiment are largely pointless. The results will almost certainly emphasise the prejudicial nature of your depressive beliefs, as well as involving you in activities that are likely to increase your sense of mastery. Have a look at the chart below for an illustration of how your NATs and assumptions can provide the foundation for useful tests of your beliefs.

Depressive assumption	Domain	Experiment	Hypotheses: if true then...
'I am no good to anybody'	SELF/ FUTURE	Undertake a morning's voluntary work for a local charity.	I will be unable to master the relevant skills. My contribution will be deemed worthless by my supervisor and fellow volunteers.
'Everyone is utterly selfish these days'	WORLD	Ask strangers in town for directions. Ask to borrow a mobile to make an emergency call.	People will refuse to help me.
'An employer would never look twice at me'	FUTURE	Go to job centre and talk to an adviser. Apply for advertised posts that match interests and experience.	Job centre adviser will confirm my opinion. I will be unsuccessful in all my applications.

3 Exercise

Some studies suggest that regular aerobic exercise for 20 minutes three times a week is as effective in relieving depression as the most common antidepressants. The reason for this is that exercise releases more serotonin, the 'feel good' hormone into your body. Antidepressants also work by keeping your serotonin levels elevated and stopping the body reabsorbing them. Exercise is also good for your self-esteem. Not only does it give you the chance to see yourself achieving the manageable short-term goals you

> regular exercise boosts energy levels by making your body more efficient

have set yourself as part of your fitness programme, but regular exercise boosts energy levels by making your body more efficient. You are also taking care of yourself, something that many depressed people find quite alien and, depending on which activity you pursue, sport may also encourage you to get out of the house and spend time with other people.

There are many, many forms of physical activity and even if you can't picture yourself on the treadmill at the local gym you will almost certainly be able to find a form of exercise that suits you. Obviously, if you are new to exercise then do get the green light from your GP before you start your training for that marathon. If you suffer from depression, even if you have never tried exercise before, consider giving it a go. You might surprise yourself.

CHAPTER 8

Conquering anxiety

'My gran always used to say to me: "You never know what's round the next corner, Em," and she's right. You can think everything's fine but fate can pull the rug from right out under you and your whole world can fall apart – just like that.'

'Every morning when I wake up the first thing I do is go through my list: "Who have I let down? What have I forgotten...?"'

'Until I started therapy I never realised how wound up I was the whole time. That sick feeling in your stomach, pacing around, constantly waiting for the next thing to go wrong... It just becomes normal after a while because you never know any different. Your brain never stops working. You're never at peace. It's hell and you don't even realise you're in it.'

What is anxiety?

People who suffer from anxiety share two things in common: they overestimate the danger inherent in situations and underestimate their ability to cope with it. Living under the shadow of the constant threat – real or imagined – has all sorts of consequences, both psychological and physically.

One of the things that fear does to our bodies is prime them for action. Hormones released into your bloodstream put you instantly into a state of red alert. You start breathing more rapidly in order to oxygenate your blood which is swiftly diverted to the muscles by your rapidly beating heart. Body systems not likely to be needed to cope with the immediate threat, like digestion, are shut down while sugar supplies stored in the liver are broken down to provide a potentially life-saving burst of energy. Your senses are sharpened while mentally all your attention is focused on the perceived threat. In this state of arousal you are now ready either to fight off the threat or leg it to safety as fast as possible.

Of course when our ancestors' daily survival depended on keeping off the menu of local predators the ability to shift into this state of heightened arousal at a moment's notice was really useful. However, the fight–flight response is designed to be a short-term measure. Neither body nor mind fare well if the state of anxious arousal is sustained over long periods.

Physically, anxiety can put you at greater risk of heart disease, stomach disorders, obesity and respiratory problems. In time it also weakens your immune system. Prolonged exposure to cortisol, one of the anxiety hormones, can even produce shrinkage in a certain region of your brain. Psychologically prolonged anxiety can make it hard to concentrate and remember things. Stress hormones leave you feeling 'on edge', exhausted and make you snappy and irritable.

Checklist of common anxiety symptoms

☐ Breathlessness

☐ Palpitations and erratic heart beat

☐ Trembling

☐ Sweating

☐ Choking sensations or finding it hard to swallow

☐ Nausea

☐ Feeling dizzy or unsteady

☐ Hot flushes

☐ Fears of going crazy or losing control

☐ Fears of dying

☐ Dissociation – feeling detached, out of touch or 'unreal'

Anxiety can manifest itself in a number of different forms. Among the diagnosable anxiety disorders are:

- **Panic disorder** People who suffer from this condition are vulnerable to acute anxiety attacks that feature several of the symptoms listed above. These intense attacks usually last for several minutes. In the CBT model of panic disorder, sufferers catastrophically misinterpret the physical and psychological effects of anxious arousal and convince themselves that something must be seriously wrong with them. This then makes their physical symptoms worse and keeps the whole cycle lurching forward.

- **Social phobia** Socially phobic people become highly anxious about the negative judgements of other people. Their fears usually focus around the evaluation of their own social performance. They may worry about blushing, stumbling over their words, or being perceived as stupid or awkward in some way. Socially phobic people fear humiliation – but their attempts to safeguard themselves against this possibility often end up working against them.

- **Agoraphobia** This is not just fear of open spaces. Agoraphobics feel at risk when they are away from the people or places that they associate with safety. They usually picture themselves getting into trouble in public places where there is no one familiar to help them or where panic symptoms could lead to public humiliation. As a result, going out becomes difficult and many agoraphobics restrict themselves by leading highly reclusive lives.

- **Obsessive Compulsive Disorder (OCD)** This is a condition that involves irrational intrusive thoughts or frightening impulses. To manage their anxiety many OCD sufferers develop compulsive rituals or checking behaviours that they pursue in attempts to neutralise their anxiety. Unfortunately the more they give themselves over to their compulsions, the worse their symptoms become. They often become convinced that unless they perform their safety rituals (such as hand washing, or counting up to 10 before they go through a door) terrible consequences will ensue. This can make it very difficult for people with OCD to give up the compulsions on which they have come to rely but which actually end up controlling their lives.

- **Specific phobias** These are irrational fears of particular things that may operate as a focus for other underlying anxieties. *Arachnophobia* (fear of spiders) is a common specific phobia. Some psychologists argue that we are more easily conditioned to become fearful of aspects of the environment that might be associated with health risks. However, it is hard to understand some of the more exotic phobias, such as *sesquippedaliophobia* (the rather cruelly entitled fear of long words) within the context of such an explanation. The truth is we can develop a phobia about almost anything. Sometimes we learn our phobic responses from other people. People who suffer from atypical phobias often struggle because it is hard for non-sufferers to take their anxieties seriously, but depending on the nature of the phobia concerned the condition can be extremely limiting.

- **Post Traumatic Stress Disorder (PTSD)** People who have experienced life-threatening or violent events can suffer intrusive recollections of the event, often in the form of flashbacks. PTSD sufferers try to avoid anything associated with the original trauma and experience a range of other anxiety symptoms including low mood, emotional numbing, irritability and concentration problems.

- **Generalised Anxiety Disorder (GAD)** This is a state of persistent worry and arousal that lasts over a period of at least six months. There are no panic attacks, obsessions or phobias involved but the sufferer usually worries about many different things – so much so that the levels of anxiety interfere with his or her ability to conduct life as normal. People with GAD are particularly prone to anticipating danger and negative outcomes to an unrealistic degree.

One in 10 of us will suffer from an anxiety disorder at some point during our lives. Severe stress can damage relationships, ruin careers and wreck lives. It is worth getting on top of, and CBT offers a number of strategies for doing just that.

Why do people suffer from anxiety?

We often refer to people as 'born worriers' and it certainly does appear to be the case that some of us have a genetic predisposition towards anxiety. We know that if one identical twin has an anxiety problem the chances of the other twin also suffering from anxiety may be as high as 88% although some studies have found much lower rates and you cannot rule out the influence of the environment that both twins have shared. The character trait labelled neuroticism is associated with worry and the area of the primitive emotional forebrain designed to react quickly to potential danger appears to be particularly responsive in people who score high on the neuroticism scales. The neurologist Klaus Peter Lesch likens such individuals to fire detectors pre-set to go off at the merest suggestion of smoke.

> The character trait labelled neuroticism is associated with worry

Environmental factors also seem to play a part. There seems to be strong evidence that certain messages given in childhood can predispose people towards anxiety by forging unhelpful core beliefs and dysfunctional assumptions.

Children of parents who are critical, rejecting or who have conveyed the message that the world is a treacherous and dangerous place are more likely to experience anxiety symptoms in adult life. If you haven't been brought up in a family that welcomes the expression of emotion and you have been taught to repress difficult feelings, then you are also more likely to be vulnerable.

Triggers

If background anxiety levels are high, one stressful life event may be all it takes to precipitate an anxiety syndrome. Just as in the cognitive model of depression, these events can activate buried beliefs about not being able to cope. Be aware that if any of the following top 10 most stressful events are taking place in your life you may need to take extra care of yourself, even though your circumstances will make it hard for you to motivate yourself to do so.

Top ten life stressors

- Death of a partner
- Divorce and separation
- Time in prison
- Death of close family member
- Injury and illness

- Getting married
- Getting fired
- Domestic conflict
- Retirement
- Pregnancy

What you will notice from this list is that some of the most stressful things that can happen to us are usually considered happy events such as marriage and pregnancy! Change is intrinsically stressful, because new situations demand more of us. We can no longer rely on automatic pilot. We are in uncharted waters and have to keep our wits about us. It is not difficult to understand how this kind of uncertainty, combined with high demands on our processing abilities, can trigger the same kind of arousal as a threat to our wellbeing.

Physiological changes that mimic the effects of anxiety can also set the anxiety response in motion. Stimulants like caffeine or drugs like amphetamines can make anxiety symptoms worse. Some physical health conditions such as hyperthyroidism or low blood sugar levels can also exaggerate latent anxiety responses which is why it is important to consult a doctor before assuming that your 'anxiety' is necessarily psychologically driven.

Maintaining factors in anxiety conditions

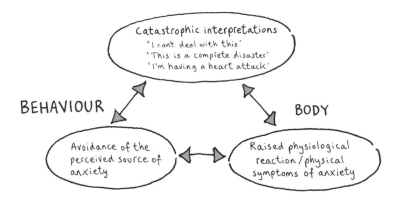

As the diagram above illustrates, the anxiety cycle is kept going by the mutual interaction of three main factors, and cognitive behavioural interventions work by addressing each of the three links in the chain.

Getting physical

'An anxious mind cannot exist in a relaxed body.'

Edmund Jacobson, doctor and creator of the progressive
relaxation method

The processes that catapult us into a state of red alert are largely automatic, and they happen so instantaneously that they can be hard to control. We have already referred to the research that suggests anxious people have a hair trigger response when it comes to anxious arousal. However, the body does have its own mechanisms for bringing itself down from the fight–flight state and returning things to normal. This is the parasympathetic nervous system, and the good news is that it is possible to harness this system to bring levels of arousal down using relaxation strategies.

One thing you can learn to do is consciously reverse some of the typical physical changes that take place in the anxious arousal state. You will have noticed that when you are anxious you tend to breathe rapidly and shallowly from the upper chest. This is because this is the most efficient way to oxygenate your muscles. However, when we are in a relaxed state we tend to breathe slowly and deeply

> when you are anxious
> you tend to breathe
> rapidly and shallowly

from the diaphragm in a regular, effortless rhythm. Practising diaphragmatic breathing when you are anxious sends a powerful signal to the parasympathetic nervous system.

brilliant tip

Harness the power of breathing

Next time you feel stress levels escalating, simply take five controlled breaths through your nose as slowly as possible, drawing the air deep into your lungs and taking time to exhale until you can expel no more air. It is the sustained out-breath that is actually more critical than the inhalation phase.

This is often sufficient to kick start a cycle of diaphragmatic breathing that, over the course of five minutes or so, should help bring your anxiety level down. Combine it with mentally picturing yourself in a beautiful, relaxing place and the effects will be even more pronounced. I know this sounds too simple to be true, but if you practise the technique it does work.

Check that you are breathing from the diaphragm by placing a hand on your stomach just below your rib cage. You should feel your stomach gently push out as you breathe in. Some people find it helpful to imagine they are sitting in front of a lit candle and that their task is to keep the flame moving slightly using their breath without putting it out.

The other physical manifestation of anxiety that it is relatively easy to undo is the muscle tension that accompanies it. Anxious people hold themselves taut and deliberately relaxing your muscles again sends the signal to both body and mind that the danger is past. There are several ways you can achieve this including progressive muscle relaxation and autogenic training.

Progressive muscle relaxation

Paradoxically you can trigger a relaxation response by racking up the tension in various muscle groups until your natural instinct is to release them. Work your way round your body scrunching up the major muscles groups in turn really tightly for a few seconds before letting go. When you do release them try to let them go completely floppy and limp. Be aware that tension often gathers in the neck and shoulders so make sure you hunch your shoulders up as far as they will go before releasing them. When you do release your muscles, mentally picture tension draining from your body as you do so. Again this takes practice, but in trials subjects who practised regularly experienced a number of beneficial effects including decrease in their anxiety levels, reduction in the frequency and intensity of panic attacks and improved concentration. You can find the full protocol for progressive relaxation at http://socialanxiety disorder.about.com/od/copingwithsad/qt/pmr.htm.

Autogenic training

In the 1930s psychiatrist Johannes Schultz found that some of his patients were able to put themselves into a light trance state simply by thinking about sensations of warmth and heaviness radiating through their bodies. Practised daily, autogenic training can produce a deep relaxation response that, once established, can be cued on demand. Autogenic training instructions and a link to a free MP3 download can be found at: http://socialanxiety disorder.about.com/od/copingwithsad.qt.autogenic.htm.

Facing your fears

'One ought never to turn one's back on a threatened danger and try to run away from it. If you do that, you will double the danger. But if you meet it promptly and without flinching, you will reduce the danger by half.'

Winston Churchill

One of the main problems for anxious people is that we have a perfectly natural tendency to avoid the source of our fears. This may seem like a good idea but, as with all safety behaviours, there is a catch. Every time you avoid a perceived threat you unwittingly reinforce the notion that there is some very good reason for keeping out of its way. This belief then confirms in your mind that the threat is genuine with the result that next time you encounter a similar situation you are even more likely to get worked up.

Furthermore, if you run from the threat – either physically or mentally – you never get the opportunity to allow your state of anxious arousal to subside in its presence and allow your body to unlearn its fear response. The fact is that if you can just stick around for long enough in the presence of your fear your anxiety symptoms will subside.

The body cannot sustain its state of acute arousal for more than a few minutes. Panic burns itself out because it gears the body for a short, intensive burst of activity. It becomes acute over the course of a few minutes and then will hit a biological ceiling before automatically subsiding. Because anxiety symptoms are so unpleasant it seems completely counterintuitive to stay put in a situation that is causing them to escalate, but actually it is one of the most effective things you can do. Exposure is a cornerstone of CBT treatment for many anxiety disorders including phobias, panic, PTSD and OCD.

> exposure is a cornerstone of CBT treatment for many anxiety disorders

brilliant technique

Work your way up the ladder of fear

By definition, this means exposing yourself to the thing you fear is going to be difficult, even if rationally you know you are perfectly safe. To make things easier psychologists often encourage people to embark on a programme of *graded exposure*. This means rather than throwing yourself in the deep end you break down confronting your fear into a series of more manageable steps.

Start by thinking of the two extremes of the scale: a situation likely to produce the most unbearable level of anxiety you can imagine (say letting a large spider crawl on your hand - fear factor rating 10+) and a situation or activity still related to your anxiety but that

▶

you are fairly confident you can manage with only minimal discomfort (maybe saying the word 'spider' out loud five times or looking at a stylised picture of one in a children's book – fear factor rating 2). Then you need to work out a series of intermediate stages ranked in order of their stress-inducing potential. By the time you have done this you will have 10 or so progressive stages that take you up towards your ultimate objective.

Don't worry if at this point you cannot begin to imagine yourself doing some of the tasks on the higher rungs of the ladder. The beauty of graded exposure is that you take it a step at a time, and you don't proceed to the next rung until you are entirely comfortable with the stage before. I cannot stress this enough. Some people find it tempting to rush through their hierarchy to 'get it over with' like gulping down a foul-tasting medicine. This is just another form of avoidance and it won't help you. The whole point of graded exposure is that you have to sit with the anxiety long enough for it to subside. If you can hang in there it will happen. As you become confident and comfortable with each level, it will make the next step possible.

It is important to bear in mind that avoidance can take many forms. It is not just a question of physically keeping yourself away from situations associated with danger. We may also avoid the things we fear by mentally blocking them out or distracting ourselves when unwanted thoughts about them intrude into consciousness. This is not a helpful strategy because attempting to suppress thoughts usually only makes them stronger.

In fact the opposite approach can be useful for some people. Deliberately inviting the feared scenario into your mind and accepting the feelings that it generates rather than fighting them is a valid form of exposure that can help desensitise you to the fear. *Imaginal exposure* is a good starting point for people who are struggling with the prospect of physically exposing themselves to the source of their anxieties. The technique is as follows:

 **technique**

Imaginal exposure

● Prepare by writing down a paragraph describing your feared scenario or the next step in your hierarchy of fear. It may be helpful to record what you have written onto CD or other recording device. Try to create a detailed and vivid description: a vague or abstract description will simply allow you to carry on avoiding.

● Get yourself into a state of physical relaxation using breathing, visualisation or another technique that works for you.

● Spend 15 minutes reading the paragraph over to yourself, vividly picturing the feared scenario in your mind.

● Accept the physical symptoms of anxiety that will start to develop but notice also how your anxiety levels tend to drop back down as you persist with the process.

● Repeat until exposure to the feared situation no longer evokes a significant anxiety response.

Anxious thinking

Situation	Emotions (%)	Automatic thoughts
Late for meeting	Fearful 70%	*I'll probably be sacked.*
	Tense 40%	*I'll never make partner now.*
	Vulnerable 30%	*Everyone will see how hot and flustered I am: I will be a laughing stock.*

Situation	Emotions (%)	Automatic thoughts
Notice a scratch on new kitchen floor	Stressed 90% Angry 10% Frustrated 70%	*It's totally ruined – why can nothing ever just go right? The flooring people saw me coming... they knew they could get away with it.*
See a police car parked in the street	On edge/nervous 60% Feeling of foreboding 80%	*Something terrible has happened. What if someone has broken into my house? Picture policemen on own doorstep breaking the news that partner has been involved in a fatal accident.*

These thought record sheets kept by Alex, a 27-year-old website designer, illustrate several of the classic thinking errors of anxious people.

The hallmark of the anxious thinking style is *catastrophising*. Anxious people keep themselves in a state of anxious arousal by continually *overestimating* the danger they are in, and *underestimating* their capacity to deal with it. Much anxious thinking is consequently oriented towards the future in which the anxious person is at liberty to populate it with terrifying scenarios.

anxious people don't actually pursue anxiety scenarios to their logical conclusion

A tell-tale sign of such thinking is the presence of NATs that begin '*What if...?*' However, one of the problems with anxious individuals is that they don't actually pursue their anxiety scenarios through to their logical conclusion. They get frozen by the prospect of how things might go wrong. They seldom take stock and appreciate that even if the worst happened (which is probably unlikely) they are not completely helpless and would have to deal with the situation as best they could. If you suffer from anxiety try to replace 'what if?' thinking with 'what then?' However uncomfortable it makes you, try to follow your anxious scenario through.

If your partner did die you probably would be devastated initially. Your grief might incapacitate you for several months and you might carry on missing your partner intensely for years. But your friends would support you, and those insurance policies would mean that you and the children would be financially secure. Eventually you would pick up the threads of your life again, drawing on the same coping skills that you have used in other contexts. Unthinkable though it might be, you might even meet someone else.

The point is that life would go on. Terrible and tragic events do happen to people from time to time, but dealing with the reality of them is often easier than dealing with the fantasy.

- Rather than trying to block out the feared scenario ask yourself: 'What is the very worst that could happen in this situation?'
- Think practically about how you would have to manage in this eventuality. What resources do you have? Who would support you?
- Relate the situation to other difficulties that you have survived and dealt with in your life. Are there any transferable skills that would help you deal with the new crisis?

 brilliant technique

What are the odds?

For anxious people their associated level of fear makes the possibility of a bad thing happening feel like a certainty to them. This *emotional reasoning* results in them miscalculating the odds of impending disaster.

▶

One technique that helps people to deal with this distortion is to break the situation down and think about the likelihood of all the separate elements that have to be in place for the unwanted outcome to occur.

If you suffer from health anxiety you might feed your fear by constantly picturing yourself in the terminal stages of cancer. But in order for this image to become true what would have to be in place or what would have to be true? These are the *necessary conditions* of your belief:

1   I would have to contract cancer in the first place.

2   The strain of cancer I contract would have to be a potentially fatal kind.

3   It would have to prove untreatable or resistant to treatment.

Using the appropriate research you could reliably establish the separate risk of each of these conditions. The probability of the only pathway that takes you to your imagined deathbed scene is the likelihood of each of the separate elements multiplied together. If you express the probabilities as fractions then the more you multiply together the smaller the end fraction (and hence percentage) becomes.

Fear of fear

For many, anxiety is maintained through a process of constant, anxious self-talk, but psychologists have also discovered recently that dysfunctional beliefs about the nature of a person's reactions to anxiety can be a significant maintaining factor in itself.

For example, if I tell myself continually *how awful* it would be to re-experience my anxiety I am even less likely to confront the immediate source of my fear. Sufferers often elaborate such dysfunctional assumptions by developing exaggerated beliefs that they will not be able to cope with symptoms or that their anxiety will drive them mad.

These beliefs about one's own thought processes are called *meta-cognitive beliefs* and if you suffer from anxiety you need to be aware of them. They could be holding you back.

Develop a stress-busting lifestyle

'Stress is what happens to us when we perceive our available resources to be insufficient to meet the demands of our circumstances.'
Richard Lazarus, academic and psychologist

Stress is cumulative, and if it is building at a rate faster than your body and mind can deal with it then eventually you will reach a point of meltdown and start to experience anxiety symptoms. Repeated low-level stressors such as squabbling children or too much noise and stimulation can have as much long-term impact as a more immediately stressful event like a road accident or losing your job. Keep an eye on the niggling stressors in your life as well as trying to protect yourself from major traumas.

> keep an eye on the niggling stressors in your life

Managing anxiety successfully cannot be done without attending to the bigger picture. Adequate rest, a healthy diet and keeping oneself in good physical shape are all protective factors against anxiety disorders. Rushing around trying to cope with multiple demands on our time and attention is a recipe for poor mental health. Unfortunately, the pace of modern life is such that it is hard to avoid being overloaded by a barrage of excessive stimuli. Learning to meditate, developing a yoga or t'ai chi practice, or simply making sure you carve out time to do some of the things that you enjoy will strengthen your resilience and improve your quality of life. Anxious people often feel far too flustered and out of control to prioritise such activities, but of course the reality is that they are precisely the ones who would most benefit from taking more care of themselves.

The advice is simple and I am sure not new to you, but reading the advice and putting it into practice are very different things. When you have finished this chapter why not sit down and contract with yourself to make one practical change to your lifestyle that you have been putting off until now?

CHAPTER 9

Taming anger

'Anybody can become angry, that is easy; but to be angry with the right person, and to the right degree, and at the right time, and for the right purpose, and in the right way, that is not within everybody's power and is not easy.'

Aristotle

As Aristotle's words imply, there is a legitimate place for anger in our lives. Anger is a natural emotional response and serves us well in many ways: well-regulated anger helps us protect ourselves when attacked, can motivate us to act decisively or act as a pressure valve to let us restore our equilibrium. However, when it rules us, anger becomes a very negative force indeed.

CBT has proved extremely useful in helping many people who struggle with anger understand the links between their behaviour and the biased ways in which they view themselves and the world around them. Because anger can so quickly cause us to lose control, the process of challenging the thoughts and attitudes that ignite rage and modifying behaviours that fuel the flames is not easy. However, it can be done and CBT can help.

How to get yourself really worked up

The inner thoughts of angry people are usually littered with distortions, but two main features stand out.

Angry people are mind readers *par excellence*. They spend a great deal of time making assumptions about what other people are thinking, and the attributions they make often imply hostile intent, selfishness or neglect on the part of the other person.

On top of this angry people stay angry because they take everything personally: their beliefs tell them that the other person is out to get them, to cheat them, to ignore their feelings or hurt them in some way. They will use massively emotive language to give form to their thoughts. They then use selective perception to gather evidence to support their beliefs and the more plausible their assumptions become, the angrier they feel.

 exercise　　What's making Malcolm mad?

Look at the example below and see whether you can identify the thought distortions responsible for building this business traveller's rage:

Malcolm has just got off the red-eye flight from New York and is at the airport waiting for his luggage to arrive. The baggage carousel has been churning slowly round for the past 20 minutes. Other people have collected their bags but Malcolm's have yet to appear.

> 'I've paid rip-off prices to travel business class for Pete's sake: surely that ought to count for something. I shouldn't be kept waiting like this...'

Malcolm can feel his temperature rising. In his mind he pictures the baggage handlers throwing his luggage around in a cavalier fashion so preoccupied with their discussion of last night's cup final that they have sent his bags trundling off to Timbuktu.

> 'It's so bloody typical of this lame-duck company! That sour-faced cow who checked me in was really offhand as well. Would it have cost her to smile? And the slop they served up – no wonder I've

*got indigestion. People just don't take any pride in their work any more. Nobody gives a damn. **@!! ing idiots! One thing's for sure: someone's going to pay for this...'*

The knot in Malcolm's stomach tightens as he feels resentment building inside him. The throbbing in his temples is becoming more and more intense.

'And who's that joker smirking at me behind his desk? Thinks it's funny does he? I bet he just loves to see us all waiting around like stranded sheep. Well I'm not standing for it. Let's see how amusing he finds it when I give him a piece of my mind...'

Malcolm storms off to harangue the airport official who innocently smiled at him, oblivious to the fact that his bags have finally arrived.

Although you may feel reading this that our traveller's anger is partially justified, those of you who have been paying attention will have noticed a number of negative assumptions and thought distortions at work in his inner rant that turn his delay from an inconvenience into a violation of his human rights.

Not only does Malcolm use highly *emotive language and imagery* to portray his experience but immediately starts seeking someone to blame for it. Underlying his response are *rigid assumptions* about what he is entitled to, and the hostile motivations of the ground crew. He searches around for evidence to support his belief (*selective perception*) that the airline is committed to providing a substandard service, *generalising* from localised instances of their apparent failings. Most of all, he makes liberal use of *mind reading* and fills in the gaps with his own negative attributions when little solid evidence about the intentions and feelings of others is available. So what is making Malcolm mad? The answer ultimately is Malcolm himself.

↗ **exercise**   Follow-up

On the same flight was Pierre, a more laid-back French executive of many years experience. He too has been standing round the carousel for the past 20 minutes but, unlike Malcolm, is in a calm and collected state. In fact he is in quite a good mood.

Can you speculate how Pierre might be framing the same situation to himself? How do his observations and explanations contrast with those of Malcolm?

Better out than in?

'It takes tremendous energy to keep our instinctual life buried and the longer and more deeply it is buried the more demonic it becomes and the more energy is required to keep it buried.'

Hal and Sidra Stone, psychotherapists

Repression is seldom a very sensible strategy when it comes to your feelings and when dealing with anger it can be disastrous. Pent up rage seeps out into our lives in a variety of distorted forms.

Nevertheless, the supposedly cathartic venting of anger may not be the way to go either. In controlled studies researchers have found that giving yourself over to your anger and 'getting it out there' by beating cushions, screaming and other such techniques, in the long term tended to increase aggressive impulses and behaviour. CBT of course would suggest that if we allow ourselves to behave like an angry person then the chances are we will soon be thinking and feeling like one too, so this makes sense. However, given that the fight–flight response does gear us for action it does follow that some kind of physical release of anger may be beneficial once in a while.

The key, of course, to managing anger well is to articulate your feelings in a controlled way and preferably long before they take you to breaking point. One of the maintaining factors for many angry people is that they don't address their feelings until way too late. Sometimes this is because they do not notice them. If you have learned to repress anger in childhood then you may brush aside small annoyances so automatically that you become unaware of the cumulative pressure building inside.

> articulate your feelings in a controlled way

For other people their past experiences and beliefs about their anger – that if expressed it will bring the world crashing down, that they will lose control, or that they will be punished or shunned – act as a powerful brake on the expression of their feelings. The repression of feeling becomes a safety behaviour that ultimately leads to the very scenario it seeks to avert when the damn bursts.

brilliant tip

Are your beliefs about your anger holding you back?

Tackling your beliefs about your anger may be just as much of a priority as addressing the content of your angry thoughts.

How strongly do you believe any of the following?

☐ I cannot control my anger. It is too powerful for me.

☐ It's wrong to feel anger.

☐ Anger should never be expressed.

☐ I must never upset other people.

☐ If I say what I feel I will be punished in some way.

▶

☐ Anger is always unacceptable.

☐ If I feel angry then it is probably my fault.

If you hold any of these beliefs use the techniques in Chapter 4 to consider alternative positions and evaluate them using Socratic reasoning.

 insight

Inflexible people are more likely to snap

The other distinctive feature of angry people is the *rigidity* of their thinking. They tend to be very dogmatic in their attitudes and their inner world is governed by innumerable rules that are often expressed in the form of 'must' and 'should' statements. To the person prone to anger their beliefs often seem self-evident: of course people should never swear; it's obvious that people who claim unemployment benefit are scrounging off the state; it stands to reason that there is always a *right* way and a wrong way to do most things.

Angry people are often highly invested in their rules and assumptions about how the world ought to be, and how it ought to treat them. Consequently, when their rules are ignored or violated by others they tend to feel assaulted. *Polarised thinking* feeds anger because it makes it hard for people who think this way to 'agree to disagree' or see things from another person's perspective. Inflexibility predisposes people towards conflict and conflict inevitably fuels aggression.

Five beliefs you may need to challenge

There are some dysfunctional assumptions that crop up repeatedly when working with people who are victims of their anger. If any of these apply to you then take the time to work through them. Weigh them against any available evidence, consider how helpful these beliefs are for you and conduct experiments to see what happens if you stop basing your actions and responses on them.

- *Everything should always be just the way I want it.*
- *All human beings are intrinsically selfish.*
- *People who don't agree with me are wrong.*
- *I must never back down or lose face.*
- *Some acts are unforgivable.*

The mind–body connection

Thinking angry thoughts puts your blood pressure up, releases adrenaline into your bloodstream and produces a keyed up state that your body interprets as proof of imminent danger. You may have suspected you were under attack in some way: now your body is confirming it for you. A feedback loop is set up almost guaranteed to keep the pressure building.

Lack of sleep, chronic stress, use of stimulants or a sugary diet that sends your metabolism fluctuating between unpredictable energy highs and crashing lows are all going to weaken your resistance to anger. Learning to relax properly (see Chapter 8) is probably one of the most helpful skills you can teach yourself if you are prone to sudden flare-ups.

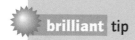 **tip**

Learn to recognise your body's anger signature

One of the problems with anger is that, unlike anxiety and depression that tend to have a longer lead-time, anger can be ignited almost instantaneously. Adrenaline is a fast-acting hormone designed to catapult the body into action in a crisis, so if you are prone to outbursts of anger you only have a few seconds in which to intervene if you want to stay in control. It is therefore particularly important that you learn to recognise the physical signals that let you know an explosion is imminent. Each person is different, but common warning signs include:

- churning sensation in the stomach
- field of vision closes in: 'the red mist descends'
- muscle tension – particularly in jaw, hands and shoulders
- automatically adopting an aggressive body stance
- hot flushes
- throbbing in the temples
- headaches
- rapid blinking or fixed staring
- accelerating heart rate
- blood rushing in the ears.

Take a moment to think about how your own body responds when you get angry. Or next time you find yourself getting riled, try to observe anger's physical effects. In particular, try to detect the very first changes, because these are the warning signs to which it will pay to be attuned.

Establish what pushes your buttons

Forewarned is forearmed and in the case of anger it is crucial to know what is likely to set you off. Keep a diary for a couple of weeks and see whether you can pull out common themes from the situations that appear to prime your anger.

- Do you get angry when you feel helpless?
- Do you get angry when other people don't appear to be listening to what you have to say?
- Do you get angry when you make mistakes?
- Do you get angry when you feel threatened?
- Do you get angry with particular people? What is it about them that gets you going?
- Can you spot any other factors that predispose you towards anger? Are you more vulnerable at certain times in the day? When you're tired? When you drink alcohol or use drugs?

Plan ahead

The point of familiarising yourself with situations likely to trigger your anger and the physical sensations and thoughts that accompany your rage is so that you can be mentally prepared when you encounter events and people likely to provoke you. You are much more likely to stay in control if you have already rehearsed how you will respond.

As you formulate and use the techniques in Chapters 2 to 4 to combat your anger-inducing attitudes you should naturally gain more spontaneous control. However, until that process starts paying dividends you might want to try some of the following more immediate CBT strategies.

The emergency anger toolbox

1 *When you spot the signs make an excuse and find the nearest exit*

Anger is a highly context-driven emotion. Take yourself out of the provoking situation and it is likely to subside. Rather than fight you will have beaten a strategic retreat, but either response is likely to satisfy the body's fight–flight drive. However, you have to act fast at the first signs of trouble.

2 *If you can't physically remove yourself, mentally detach yourself*

Decentre yourself by observing your own thoughts and the sensations that your boiling emotions create in you. Use your imagination to zoom out and give yourself a bird's eye view of the situation from a corner of the ceiling or from a safe distance.

3 *Make yourself untouchable*

If another person is triggering your anger then rather than internally bracing yourself against them try visualising yourself in a smooth protective bubble while their barrage of annoying words glides effortlessly past as if you were standing in a slipstream.

4 *Do a quick cost/benefit analysis*

Consider the likely consequences of losing your rag at this juncture. Are you prepared to pay the price for losing control? Has getting angry been a productive response for you in the past? Will you feel more or less self-respect once the moment has passed? Not only will this process distract you from the immediate provocation but it will keep the rational side of you engaged so you won't yield yourself completely to the primitive emotion-driven centres of the forebrain.

5 *Suck on a sweet!*

This is a tip I owe to a psychologist called Dr Doyle Gentry. Although it sounds ridiculous it often works quite powerfully.

Your knowledge of CBT may give you some clues as to why. Firstly, the act of sucking gives you a sensate focus to direct your attention away from your fury. It's a distraction and breaks cycles of aggressive rumination. Secondly, sucking is a primitive reflex associated with our earliest experiences of nurture and comfort. Because of the behaviour–feelings connection having something sweet-tasting in your mouth can activate feelings of wellbeing and relaxation that are incompatible with the emotions fuelling your annoyance.

6 Take some slow deep breaths

Very basic, but diaphragmatic breathing does trigger the parasympathetic nervous system responsible for calming you down when you are in a highly charged or agitated state. It doesn't work right away though: you need to breathe slowly and calmly for a good few minutes before it will take effect. Counting can help slow your breathing down. If you hyperventilate your breathing will have the opposite effect biologically and emotionally and leave you feeling even more wound up.

Savage Chickens   by Doug Savage

www.savagechickens.com

Why improved communication skills can help you stay in control

We will return to the principles of assertive communication in the next chapter that deals with low self-esteem, but angry people often benefit enormously from these skills. Learning how to express your annoyance before it turns into rage, and that it is legitimate to ask people to respect your feelings, often makes a huge difference. The benefits for the angry person are many:

- Open communication can clear up misunderstandings and misconceived assumptions about what others are thinking.

- Assertiveness skills are empowering and therefore help address one of the sources of anger.

- Assertive people take responsibility for making themselves understood. This means they are less prone to irrational blame, another catalyst for anger.

- Good communication allows sustained problem solving so more constructive solutions can be found to problems and tensions that could otherwise destabilise your mood.

- You will be less likely to alienate people if you communicate assertively rather than aggressively. They will consequently be more inclined to give you what you want so your frustration levels will drop.

Getting to the roots of your anger

As we have seen anger can gather a momentum of its own but it often draws its intensity from the past. Much of the anger we express on a day-to-day basis is *displaced emotion* – in other words it may be attached to some immediate and usually trivial cause but it stems from somewhere else altogether. The attitudes and beliefs that drive anger are usually forged in childhood experience, although other formative life events may also be fuelling your rage.

Social learning theory makes the point that our own behaviour can be heavily influenced by the behaviour we observe around us. If you were brought up by *role models* who displayed excessive anger – even if not actively directed towards you – it is quite conceivable that you have unconsciously learned to imitate them. Of course the influence of the people and situations we expose ourselves to does not stop once we are older. The old proverb that we 'become like the company we keep' is psychologically astute. If you are surrounding yourself with other angry people it will be hard for you not to follow suit. Anger is a highly contagious emotion.

> our own behaviour can be heavily influenced by the behaviour we observe around us

The other question to ask yourself is whether your anger might actually belong to someone else? People who, for whatever reason, cannot deal with or articulate their own rage are often capable of *projecting* their angry feelings onto others.

In social systems like families, the individual members tend to assume different roles. Certain group members may be assigned the job of expressing emotions that other group members have disowned. All this happens at an unconscious level but children can often find themselves cast into the role of the person who emotes the feelings that other family members cannot tolerate.

This can be confusing and disturbing, because of course the person who performs this role doesn't really know why they are feeling as they do. However, once anger has a foothold in your life it can be hard to shake.

Anger can be a big and overwhelming emotion for children, an experience that can feel very threatening for them, especially if the anger is directed at a parent upon whom the child relies. Being possessed by rage can make a child feel dangerously out of control. Children are also very conscious that the adults in their world are bigger and stronger than them. On several counts, making an enemy of a grown-up can be an alarming prospect. As a result children often deal with significant anger by burying it deep inside themselves.

It is ironic that we often think of 'problem children' as the ones likely to be throwing tantrums, but on the whole children who feel safe enough to express their infuriation with the world when they are toddlers are less likely to fall prey to engrained anger problems as adults. It is indeed often the quiet ones that you need to watch.

So what do children get angry about? There are innumerable causes but here are some of the most common. As you reflect upon this list, ask yourself what kind of assumptions and core assumptions are these causes likely to foster?

Powerlessness

It is easy to forget as an adult how little real power you have when you are young. You are dependent upon those round you for your survival, and without their help you can do very little for yourself. If you are a grown-up in a situation you find intolerable you can usually do something about it but this is not the case for a child. Repeated experiences of being rendered helpless can form unhelpful core beliefs. Unpredictable or aggressive adults can reinforce a child's sense of powerlessness and the frustration that accompanies this.

Violation of rights

Children very quickly develop a sense of right and wrong, and it is no coincidence that 'it's not fair' is one of the most common complaints of childhood. Repeated exposure to situations they feel to be unjust (perhaps perceiving their sibling to be favoured above them) or in which they are subject to abuse or cruelty from others is likely to breed resentment and rage.

Traumatic experience

Anger is a self-protective instinct and is often the flipside of fear. When our survival or wellbeing is threatened, or our assumptions about the world are stood on their head by some unexpected trauma, the end result can be high levels of anxiety that can easily precipitate angry outbursts. If you don't feel safe deep down, then your insecurity can make you prone to lashing out. If you haven't dealt properly with the pain, distress and fear associated with such experiences then this is even more likely.

Constant criticism or neglect

Criticism, even if meant to be constructive, can feel like an attack. If you were a child exposed to constant disapproval and told either directly or indirectly you did not meet the standards expected of you, then the part of you that did not feel crushed may well have attempted to fight back with anger. However, if that anger was not deemed acceptable or put you at risk of further damage to your self-esteem you may well have had to repress such feelings.

Simply being ignored, or having your needs overlooked, can also feel like an assault to a child. A child who is not taken care of physically or emotionally is being given the message that she is undeserving of basic care. At some level she will register and resent this.

Narcissistic injury

It is entirely normal for children to go through periods of their development when they become extremely self-centred. During such phases they find it hard to put themselves into the shoes of others and appreciate other people's points of view. A hallmark of such phases is a massive sense of entitlement: they believe that the world should run exactly as they want and when it doesn't they feel outraged. They find it hard to tolerate any insinuation that they are less than perfect, or that the world is less than perfectly attuned to their needs and desires.

In fact such overblown conceit is usually the public face of underlying fears about not being good enough and the consequences that might follow from their imperfection. Narcissism is a brittle, anxiety-laden state characterised by many of the thinking errors linked to anger. For people who get stuck in a narcissistic position, possibly because their needs have not been adequately met, anger can quickly become a way of life.

> narcissism is a brittle, anxiety-laden state characterised by many of the thinking errors linked to anger

Dealing with predisposing factors from childhood

You obviously cannot change the past, but you can do a lot to change its influence over you. In order to do this you usually have to change the meaning or significance of past events and for most people this is a gradual process of adjustment. This book would be doing you a disservice if it implied that this could be done quickly and easily because in most cases it can't. You may even need the help of a suitable professional to help you unpack some of your childhood legacy.

If repressed feelings are driving your anger then even many years after the event it can still be surprisingly beneficial to express them. Sometimes it can be relevant and productive to express your feelings directly to the person concerned, but this becomes more complex if that person is now elderly or vulnerable in some other way, and it is not even always necessary. Writing a letter from the point of view of when you were a child is an exercise many people find genuinely helpful. Giving a voice to your repressed emotions, even on paper, can release something important. What you do with such a letter afterwards is up to you. It may or may not be appropriate to send it.

Do I have to forgive?

Clients often get to an *impasse* in therapy where they put themselves under enormous pressure to forgive some past hurt at a point when they still feel unable to do so. It is crucial to remember that forgiveness is not mandatory. See it rather as a power at your disposal, even if you are not ready to deploy it. Whether you ever choose to exercise that power is entirely up to you.

People often feel that if they forgive the offence against them they are somehow absolving the other person of responsibility, but this is not necessarily the case. What you *are* doing is resolving to stop mentally calling them to account for their crimes. You are choosing to direct your emotional resources elsewhere.

- Try to focus on the potential personal costs of choosing not to exercise your power of forgiveness: if you hold on to and continually replay NATs that promote bitterness, distress and resentment then you are going to damage yourself. If any belief does not promote your wellbeing then CBT would suggest it should be modified or dispensed with. Choose not to amplify any harm that has already been done.

- Try to describe the offender's actions and their impact upon you in the least emotive terms that you can, without compromising the truthfulness of your account. It is hard to forgive when you are still using incendiary language that supercharges your resentment.

- Make your forgiveness primarily about *you* and the person that *you* choose to become rather than the other person. Take responsibility for your own actions, even if the person who hurt you does not do the same.

 insight

Believe it or not, most of us are doing our best

Every human being is driven in everything they do by the desire to get their needs met. Within this framework we generally make the best choices we can in the light of the knowledge we have available to us at the time.

This does not mean that we always make very astute choices, or that people don't make choices that cause awful suffering to others. Sometimes we all act on the basis of priorities that in retrospect strike us as misplaced, guided by values that with the benefit of experience we may later completely repudiate.

Sometimes we are mistaken about what our true needs are, or the best way to go about meeting them: wars are fought, children are abused, terrible things happen in the world all as a result of misguided attempts to get needs met. Understanding this – while it may not excuse the harmful actions of others – can take us a step towards reframing past hurts in ways that are less psychologically damaging for us in the present. If you have made what you feel to be bad mistakes yourself, try to identify the underlying needs that you were seeking to meet at the time.

CHAPTER 10

Boosting self-esteem

'Our deepest fear is not that we are inadequate. Our deepest fear is that we are powerful beyond measure. It is our light, not our darkness that most frightens us. We ask ourselves, Who am I to be brilliant, gorgeous, talented, fabulous? Actually, who are you not to be...? Your playing small does not serve the world.'

Marianne Williamson

 **brilliant** example

'I told you I would stuff up'

Elizabeth has worked at Marston and Sons, a northern clothing manufacturer, for the past 15 years. Her highly conscientious attitude to her work was spotted and she was promoted to the position of floor supervisor seven years ago. Her manager believes that Elizabeth is talented and has pushed her to apply for a fast-track, management-training programme.

Despite her reservations, Elizabeth now stands in front of the interview panel about to give a presentation as part of the application process. Her mouth is dry and her hands are trembling. Trying to mask her nerves she switches on the overhead projector to put up her first slide. To her horror she suddenly realises that the slide on the screen is not the first in the sequence. Elizabeth is appalled. What an idiot! She was up half the night checking through the presentation and can't believe she has been so stupid. What are ▶

they going to think of her now? Clearly that she is incompetent – which she evidently is. She is definitely the very last person in the world anyone should ever give a management job to.

In her mind's eye Elizabeth can see her stepmother's disappointed face as she turns away from her, shaking her head reproachfully. She was stupid to try for this anyway. She should know her place. They told her at school that she was best suited to manual work. If only she had checked through them one more time, however tired she was... 'Practise makes perfect, Elizabeth!' That's what Mrs Jenner would say.

Elizabeth is aware that her face has turned bright red with embarrassment. She tries to speak, to apologise for the mess she has made, but no words come out. She looks blankly at the interview panel and sees nothing but stony, judgemental faces. What did she expect? Her notes drop to the floor. Unable to bear it any longer, Elizabeth bursts into tears and rushes headlong for the door.

Understanding the cycle of low self-esteem

The unfortunate Elizabeth demonstrates some of the classic traits and habits of someone with low self-esteem. You can see the way a simple mistake triggers a cascade of critical self-talk that rapidly incapacitates her both physically and mentally, unleashing overwhelming feelings of shame and worthlessness.

Elizabeth's negative self-evaluation becomes self-fulfilling. Her fixed belief that she must perform to the highest possible standard at all times to qualify for any sense of self-worth has prompted her to stay up late into the night until, exhausted, she made the error with her slides.

Having made the mistake, her persecutory thinking makes it almost impossible for her to recover. In her panic she starts to behave incompetently in front of the panel, merely confirming to herself that the critical voices from the past were right about her.

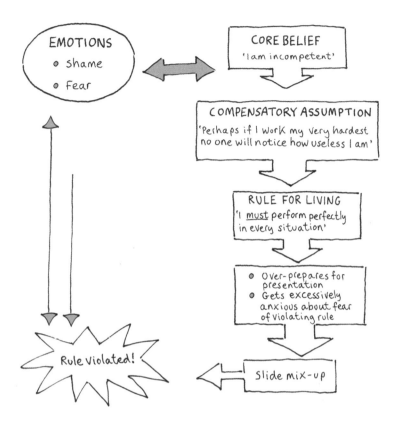

Breaking the rules

As far as the CBT model is concerned, the reason that people who suffer from a poor self-image are so vulnerable is because they cling rigidly to a set of fixed beliefs about the conditions under which they are allowed to feel okay about themselves.

When these rules are broken the individual is laid open to the full emotional consequences of latent core beliefs that they are bad, helpless or unlovable. Trying to stick to the rules is actually a safety behaviour designed to safeguard them from a toxic cocktail of distressing feelings.

trying to stick to the rules is actually a safety behaviour

However, the rules themselves are invariably so rigid and so extreme that the poor person concerned has little realistic chance of living up to their demands. When they fail to do so, they feel demoralised, ashamed and depressed and often end up behaving in ways that further damage their self-image and reinforce those negative core beliefs.

 exercise   **Are your rules helping you?**

Take a few minutes to see whether you can identify any unhelpful rules of your own. Sometimes such rules are not obvious but hidden in our assumptions and moral values. They can often be detected by the presence of the words 'should', 'ought' and 'must' but this is not always the case. They will be closely associated with your sense of right and wrong and often reflect the expectations of other people.

This is not, of course, to suggest that all moral principles and values should be thrown out as dysfunctional assumptions... The rules that cause problems for us tend to be:

- **Rigid** Such rules are absolutes. They don't take into account our individual needs or circumstances. They are usually the product of polarised thinking.

- **Inherited** Often unhelpful rules are imported wholesale from key figures in childhood. Such rules, assumptions and values have often never been examined or evaluated.

- **Unrealistic** People often impose standards on themselves that, with the best will in the world, it is not possible to uphold. You might aspire to be a kind person, but no one is kind all the time. If you have rules that insist that you are, then it is inevitable that you will fall short.

- **Restrictive** CBT ultimately enshrines a humanistic value system that holds growth, freedom and personal development as fundamental rights of every human being. If your rules stand in the way of such objectives you might want to question their role in your life. Always ask yourself: 'Are my beliefs helping me?'

As you begin to unearth your rules and values, consider each one in the light of these criteria. Here are a few examples of such rules and assumptions to stimulate your thinking:

Assumption		Rule	Criteria
I mustn't upset people	→	I must hide my feelings	☑ Rigid? ☐ Inherited? ☑ Unrealistic? ☑ Limiting?
I should always put the needs of others first	→	I must avoid saying 'no' to people	☐ Rigid? ☑ Inherited? ☐ Unrealistic? ☑ Limiting?
Sex is dirty	→	So I must never think about it or talk about it	☑ Rigid? ☑ Inherited? ☑ Unrealistic? ☑ Limiting?
Mistakes are unacceptable	→	Do my best to be faultless	☐ Rigid? ☐ Inherited? ☑ Unrealistic? ☑ Limiting?

Now see whether you can add a few of your own...

Assumption		Rule	Criteria
1	→		☐ Rigid? ☐ Inherited? ☐ Unrealistic? ☐ Limiting?
2	→		☐ Rigid? ☐ Inherited? ☐ Unrealistic? ☐ Limiting?
3	→		☐ Rigid? ☐ Inherited? ☐ Unrealistic? ☐ Limiting?
4	→		☐ Rigid? ☐ Inherited? ☐ Unrealistic? ☐ Limiting?

So how do you change the rules?

There are three things you can do to start with:

1 Remind yourself that your rules are based on beliefs and values that other people may not share so they are not set in stone. Our rules are aspects of a personal meaning system that can never be objectively 'true'. As this book has hopefully shown you by now, beliefs and meanings can be changed and adapted to better suit your needs.

2 Systematically review the evidence as to whether your rules are helpful for you and test them against the criteria listed above.

3 Conduct behavioural experiments to look at the consequences of alternative rules or see what happens if you
deliberately allow yourself to break your current ones. Do
the anticipated consequences always follow? What does it
actually feel like to live according to different principles?
Can you list the personal advantages or disadvantages of
alternative positions?

brilliant tip

Choose your own values

Avoid using the words 'should', 'must' and 'ought'. Substitute them
with phrases like 'I prefer to...', 'I choose to...' and 'I want to...'
(providing, of course, that this is actually the case!). This will help
expose implicit rules that you may wish to reconsider and help you
identify the values that you do want to uphold.

brilliant example

No more Mr Nice Guy!

Daniel was the most mild-mannered individual you could hope to meet. He
came across as a bumbling clown of a man with a shy, bashful air about
him. The son of a violent, alcoholic father, Daniel had spent his childhood
never knowing what mood his dad would be in when he came home from
the pub. He had learnt from an early age the importance of placating his
father and had subsequently generated a number of rules about how he
must always defer to others that he still lived by as an adult.

Daniel's low self-esteem had made him quite depressed and as part of an
effort to galvanise his activity levels he agreed to join the local amateur
dramatics society. The group was due to put on a production of Robin Hood
as the annual pantomime, and when another actor fell sick, Daniel had to ▶

step into the part of the evil Sheriff of Nottingham at the last minute. He was a huge success in the role, but more impressive was the change the experience produced in Daniel.

'You've no idea how weird it is for me to get inside the head of someone who just takes what he wants and doesn't give a stuff about anyone else,' he told me later. 'That's so different to how I've trained myself to be – the Dan who's always keeping the peace, always thinking about how everyone else feels... It was just the best thing. Don't get me wrong: I don't want to be a villain in real life, but it's made me realise that perhaps I've gone a little bit too far in the other direction.'

Abandoning his life-long rules, even just for a couple of hours on stage, had given Daniel an insight into a brave new world of exciting possibilities.

The origins of low self-worth

People who feel bad about themselves usually do so because they have been programmed with negative messages about themselves from an early age. These messages are not always explicit: sometimes the way children are treated drives them to conclusions about their lack of value just as surely as if someone was telling them directly to their face. It is worth briefly examining some of the ways in which negative core beliefs are laid down, because understanding their origins can equip us better to tackle them.

Neglect

Nothing says 'You're worthless' quite like ignoring your basic needs. And basic needs for children include affection and warmth as well as a roof over their heads and food on the table. Children who feel unloved or uncared for invariably conclude at some level that they are bad because otherwise surely their carers would be motivated to look after them? Because of their vulnerability and dependence upon the adults in their world – however negligent those adults might be – it is usually safer for a child to hold themselves responsible for their poor treatment rather than acknowledge that their carers are incapable or unwilling to do the job properly.

Associated beliefs:	*'I don't count.'*
	'I am unlovable.'
	'I am not good enough to be looked after.'

Trauma and abuse

When bad things happen to us it is very natural to assume we are being punished in some way, or conclude that we were not worth protecting. These assumptions can form even when we can satisfy ourselves that we have just been unlucky or that the misfortune we have suffered is not our fault. Trauma can also leave us feeling powerless, overwhelmed and unable to cope – all experiences that are at odds with a healthy self-concept.

Associated beliefs:	*'I am weak and vulnerable.'*
	'I deserve bad things to happen to me.'
	'No one kept me safe. Perhaps I don't matter.'

Failing to live up to expected standards

We have already illustrated how for some people breaking their internalised rules can precipitate a crisis of confidence about their self-worth. However, sometimes these unrealistic standards are programmed into us from an early age. Parents who place excessive expectations on their children, either in terms of their morality or performance, can put their self-esteem under enormous pressure. If they fail to meet these standards children feel (or are made to feel) bad. Even if they succeed then their self-worth is likely to feel contingent on future performance, which means ultimately it is conditional.

Associated beliefs: *'I just let everyone down.'*

'If I don't do what others want then I am worthless.'

Sustained criticism

Whatever you may feel about the merits of over-praising children, developmental psychologists have known for a long time that an environment of constant criticism erodes self-esteem more reliably than almost anything else. If you allow yourself to tune into your internal critic – and we all have one – you will most likely hear the voice of a disapproving parent. The inner monologue of people with low self-esteem is constantly reproving and condemning. If, as a child, you were constantly being taken to task then you are likely to have internalised negative attributions that, if left unchecked, can continue to damage your self-image in the present. If your carers backed up their disapproval with displays of anger or withdrawal the impact is likely to be particularly pronounced.

> if you tune into your internal critic you will most likely hear the voice of a disapproving parent

Of course it is not only our parents who can pass judgement upon us. People who belong to minority groups may well end up feeling judged by society as a whole. Growing up gay, disabled or in an ethnic minority is still far from easy in today's world and sadly members of such groups often struggle with self-esteem issues as a result of other people's perceptions of them.

Associated beliefs: *'Something's wrong with me.'*

'However hard I try I will never be good enough.'

'I am unworthy.'

Reworking formative memories

All the standard CBT approaches are relevant to dealing with core beliefs linked to self-esteem, but in addition it may be helpful to imagine setting up some kind of dialogue between yourself when you were younger and the adult you have now become.

Retrospectively changing the meaning of key past experiences is not always easy – but it is possible. You are usually dealing with the interpretations and conclusions reached by a child with far less life experience and insight than you have as an adult, so it can be helpful to think not only about how the original conclusions were drawn but whether they were valid or balanced.

Pick out some of the key experiences that moulded the child's beliefs. Having put yourself into a relaxed state try to picture the scene in as much detail as you can.

1 Run the scene through a couple of times in your imagination, trying to experience it from the child's point of view. What were the prominent features of the scene? What did the child feel at the time? What was he or she most aware of? Can you recall any thoughts or images that passed through your head back then or snatches of dialogue that seem especially significant? What sense did the child make of those experiences?

2 Now run the scene through again, this time trying to put yourself in the position of other key characters in the scene. What were they thinking and feeling? What insights can you gain into why they acted as they did?

3 Using what you have learnt, the next step is to write down three things you would have wished the child could have appreciated or understood at the time. Keep your message brief and try to keep it in the present tense. Perhaps you need the child to grasp that he or she was not responsible for what happened, or expose some of the things he or she was told and believed as untrue? Perhaps you will simply need

to affirm the child's value at a time when he or she was left feeling ashamed or stupid.

4 Finally, replay the scene one more time, but this time imagine your adult self standing at the child's side. Picture yourself explaining to the child what you now know. In your mind's eye imagine the child assimilating any new information or insights and processing the implications of your message.

brilliant example

Jemima was using this technique to reprocess a memory of being left with her grandparents in the UK while her mother and father went abroad to try to clear out their farm in Uganda before it was taken over by Idi Amin's troops. She remembered feeling desolate – not understanding why her parents had left her behind when her older brother went back home to Africa with them. She recalled how the experience had fed her insecurity about whether she was dispensable to her family. As an adult she knew rationally that the decision had been made because her parents had feared for her safety in the uncertain political climate of Uganda. However, not until she imagined herself communicating this to the seven-year-old Jemima did she begin to weaken the force of latent beliefs that she was 'unwanted' and an 'outsider' in the family. When she came round from the exercise, Jemima was slightly tearful. When asked whether she was okay she replied: 'Yes... it's just that Young Me gave Old Me a message too... I feel a bit embarrassed to say... She said she was glad that one day she would grow up to be a lady with a big handbag and pretty make-up like mine.'

Further techniques to repair your self-image

As the CBT expert Judith Beck points out, the kind of negative core beliefs that damage self-esteem can be grouped under two main headings – beliefs about being helpless and beliefs about being worthless. The interventions that CBT practitioners use when addressing low self-esteem tend to target these two basic areas.

Look after yourself

Whatever their background, people who suffer from low self-worth tend to neglect themselves in important areas of their lives. Their behaviour follows naturally on from their belief that they have little or no value: think about how you treat an expensive new car compared with your rusty old banger! Conversely, because of the two-way street principle in CBT, if you start to treat yourself as if you did have value then you will begin to steer your thinking processes and your emotions in a similar direction.

Individuals with low self-worth may not look on the surface as if they are neglecting themselves. They may even present a well-groomed appearance to the outside world, but often there will be significant areas of unmet need in the way they live their lives. Perhaps they don't prioritise rest and relaxation because they are spending all their time doing things for others. Maybe they are secretly starving or overfeeding themselves. If you are serious about tackling your self-esteem issues you need to start treating yourself as if your wellbeing mattered, even if you don't currently feel that way.

> you need to start treating yourself as if your wellbeing mattered

- Diet, exercise and adequate sleep are all part of the equation. If your wardrobe is shabby invest in some new clothes. Just don't bankrupt yourself doing so because that is not looking after yourself either! Pay attention to personal grooming, not to conform to other people's aesthetic standards but to give yourself the message that, as the corny advert would tell you, 'You're worth it...'.

- Cut back on the habits and indulgences that feel comforting but actually constitute a veiled form of self-harm: smoking, over-eating, starving yourself, spending hours in front of the telly all need to be addressed. If you really liked yourself would you be doing quite so much of any of these?

- Find healthy and constructive alternatives that give you pleasure. Lose yourself in a dance class, or treat yourself to a professional massage. Go for a walk in the countryside and listen to your favourite music. Make time to do the things you enjoy and that make you feel good.

Become an assertive communicator

Developing assertive communication skills is an important step for people with self-esteem issues. Expressing yourself clearly and directly is in itself an affirmation of self-worth. Whatever the content of your communication you are saying, in effect, that you believe that what you have to say is worth listening to, while letting the other person hog the floor or 'suffering in silence' is not the act of someone with a very strong self-belief.

Key strategies for more effective communication

- When you want to sound assertive keep it clear and concise. Less is more. Don't waffle or be tentative. This will make you sound deferential and weaken the impact of what you are saying.

- Don't be afraid to use the first person. Under-confident people are often loathe to say 'I' but owning your wishes, feelings and beliefs directly makes you sound confident and strong. Moreover no one can directly challenge you because only you are in a position to pronounce authoritatively on the contents of your own heart and mind. 'I would like to think through the proposal for a few days' is a strong, assertive statement, whereas 'Perhaps, all things considered, it would be better to think things through for a while' invites the possibility of dissent. Perhaps it wouldn't be better? Maybe it would be better to decide here and now?

- When making requests of other people use the following three-point formula:

  1 Describe the situation as you see it.

  2 Request the change you want.

  3 State any action you intend to take or consequences that will ensue if your request is not met.

  For example (after several polite attempts earlier in the evening):

  1 *'I can hear the music from your flat really loudly and it is now past midnight.'*

  2 *'I would like you to turn it down now please.'*

  3 *'If you don't I will be lodging a complaint with the council.'*

- Practise using a strong, clear voice. Don't use a whiny tone or mumble your words.

- Check your body language. Make good eye contact and plant your feet firmly on the floor. Don't fold your arms or you will look defensive. Drop your shoulders and hold your head up. The aim is to hold yourself relaxed but upright. Under-confident speakers often stoop or appear to be collapsing under the force of gravity.

- When being criticised you can often disarm your critic by not jumping to defend yourself but finding something in her comments that you can agree with, even if only in principle. This technique is called *fogging.*

- When negotiating try to work towards solutions that yield some kind of pay-off for both parties. You will get much further.

 tip

> **Remember:** assertiveness is not the same thing as aggression. Truly assertive communication is respectful of the self-esteem of everyone involved.

Don't allow yourself to be thwarted

Researchers have found that heaping praise on children is not the most effective way to promote their self-esteem. What really counts is having opportunities to experience themselves as effective and competent people. Self-esteem is synonymous with self-efficacy. On the other hand, if you allow yourself to become helpless and convince yourself you lack the resources to get your needs met, your self-esteem will suffer.

Negative beliefs about helplessness are a recurring theme for people with low self-worth. Once established, they can encourage passive and defeatist attitudes that only make the situation worse. Many people with poor self-images sit on their dreams and aspirations because they allow their critical inner voices to rob them of the possibility of turning dreams into reality. This leads to a further sense of frustration and futility that reinforces how powerless the individual has become. To break this cycle:

> negative beliefs about helplessness are a recurring theme

1 *Make a comprehensive inventory of past achievements and current skills.* You will use this to bolster your confidence and counter negative beliefs such as self-critical affirmations that you 'are incapable of ever achieve anything worthwhile' when working towards new goals becomes difficult.

2 *Set yourself some goals and plan steps towards achieving them.* Are there projects, large or small, you have always wanted to embark on but have talked yourself out of? What would you be doing if only you had the confidence? Make a list of at least five and select two objectives that you are going to work on.

3 *Break your goals into a series of smaller subgoals.* If you wanted to take up fishing your subgoals might include a trip to the library to get out some related reading and a phone call to the friend at work who offered to take you along to the local trout farm one day.

4 *Set yourself a realistic time scale and schedule for achieving your subgoals.* Don't forget to incorporate regular review points so you can monitor how your progress is coming along, factor in any new subgoals, and take action if your plans are going astray.

5 *Think about any obstacles that might present themselves* (e.g. general inertia, other people's demands on your time, your impending house move) and make specific contingency plans about how such obstacles might be managed and overcome.

6 *When you have reached your goal take time to celebrate.* This is a way of consolidating your sense of achievement and logging an experience that can be used as an effective counter to future negative thoughts about being ineffectual or powerless.

brilliant tip

Reframe your 'failures' in a more positive light

If your self-esteem is fragile it is easy to get discouraged when things don't go according to plan. However, psychologist Carol Dweck writes persuasively about the 'growth mindset' as being characterised by a preparedness to welcome mistakes and apparent failures of all kinds as a natural, valuable and inevitable part of

▶

learning. Develop the attitude of Thomas Edison, the American inventor, who was once heard to remark: 'I haven't failed. I've just found 10,000 ways that don't work.'

Try a little tenderness

As we have seen, people who suffer from low self-esteem often develop a highly critical inner voice that leaves them prone to feelings of inadequacy and shame. One of the best antidotes to these problems has turned out to be deliberately cultivating specifically compassion-based cognitions that can be highly effective in counteracting your hostile internal commentary.

Dr Paul Gilbert has found that by deliberately concentrating on generating feelings of compassion towards oneself and other people impressive changes can be achieved. In a study conducted in a high-security psychiatric hospital, a group of patients reported significant improvements in their self-esteem and the lifting of depressive symptoms after just a few weeks of compassion-based meditation.

Developing a compassionate stance towards oneself and others depends on cultivating three main attitudes:

- A willingness to be mindful and open to one's own distress rather than trying to shut it down prematurely.

- Adopting a kind and non-judgmental stance towards self and others.

- Developing an awareness of sharing feelings of suffering with others, rather than concentrating on feelings of isolation or shame.

Many of these ideas have much in common with the Mindfulness approach already being used in the treatment of a variety of mental health problems with considerable success. An important element is the preparedness to accept negative thoughts and feelings when they arise, stand back and observe them, and then allow them to subside. In Compassion Focused Therapy the techniques of CBT are used to normalise suffering and challenge assumptions that such states are intolerable or damaging. Examples of the sorts of compassion-based response we are talking about include alternative thoughts like the following:

Negative automatic thoughts	Compassion-based responses
'I can't stand this pain inside...'	'Emotional pain is an unavoidable part of life that we all must share. It is unpleasant but normal. It feels bad now but it will pass in due course. If I can accept it rather than struggle against it, it will hurt me less'
'What I've done is unforgivable. I'm just scum.'	'I can always choose to love and forgive myself, no matter what I have done or how I have acted in the past. We are all human and we all make mistakes. Although I choose to face the consequences of my actions, including how they make me feel right now, I recognise that there will come a time when I need to wipe the slate clean and start afresh.'
'I've come to the end of the road. I can't face going on anymore...'	'Right now I feel desperate, and I choose to stand back and observe my feelings, reminding myself that however terrible they may be they don't have to control me. Part of me is separate from them, just noticing them. It's a good, strong, wiser part of me that remains unaffected, whatever I may be experiencing right now.'

The science behind Compassion Focused Therapy claims that when we rehearse self-critical and negative thoughts, we activate the subsystem of our brains designed to help us deal with threat and unwittingly prime a state of arousal that primes us for fight or flight. The techniques of CFT are designed to persuade the threat-response system to stand down, by actively cueing a separate subsystem designed to soothe us and restore a sense of equilibrium by producing feelings of reassurance, comfort and safety and releasing oxytocin and endorphins into our bloodstream.

 **brilliant** tip

Be careful how you speak to yourself

Gilbert was interested in why many people using CBT techniques reported that while rationally they were convinced by their alternative thoughts, they often lacked emotional conviction. It was 'head knowledge' but it didn't seem to connect with what they felt inside. What Gilbert discovered was that often such people were using CBT to reason with themselves in quite a harsh, critical or detached way, as if they were blaming themselves for their thinking errors or simply commanding themselves to think differently. Once he persuaded them to start imagining delivering the alternative thoughts in a kind, gentle and soothing tone, many of his subjects reported finding them much more effective. This makes sense in terms of Gilbert's model: it looks as if the very thoughts that were supposed to be an antidote to negative cognitions were being administered in such a way as to trigger the threat-response system!

There are many aspects to Gilbert's Compassion-based therapy model that lie beyond the scope of this brief introduction. If you are interested in acquainting yourself further with Paul Gilbert's theories and methods, I would recommend his book *The*

Compassionate Mind. However, the notion that fostering attitudes of kindness and self-acceptance directly may be just as important in boosting our sense of self-efficacy is an important one for anyone who suffers from the symptoms of low self-esteem.

 **exercise**   A compassion-based meditation to try for yourself

You can try out a CFT technique for yourself. Seek out a quiet place where you won't be interrupted. Find a comfortable position and close your eyes. Allow yourself to imagine the most compassionate, wisest version of yourself possible. Imagine yourself sitting in a pool of beautiful pure light. Decide for yourself what colour best represents for you the quality of pure compassion and tint the light beam accordingly. In your mind's eye let the light wash over you, soaking into every fibre of your being, and gathering in your core where it grows stronger and sweeter and brighter. Notice how the light makes you feel safe, accepted, and secure. You feel completely at peace. Now imagine that the light entering you is also flowing through you and out towards the world, reaching out towards other people, irrespective of who they are or the mistakes they have made. And as the light touches them you watch them changing. Their faces soften. Their postures relax. Their movements become more fluid. They look lighter, happier, bathed in the glow of this constant stream of loving energy that finds no fault with any of them and touches the heart of each, just as surely as it calms and settles your own. Take a moment to enjoy a profound feeling of deep acceptance and connection. See yourself sitting there with the light streaming into you and out through you, connecting you to every living thing.

CHAPTER 11

Breaking
the cycle:
using CBT
to overcome
addictions and
destructive
habits

There are few of us who can't identify with the truth of the old Chinese proverb: 'Habits are cobwebs first; cables at last.' Whether our destructive habits range from trivial but annoying things like procrastination or biting your nails, to more serious problems with drugs or alcohol, we can all find ourselves locked into undesirable patterns of repeating behaviour that can undermine our quality of life. Addictive behaviour is becoming an increasing problem for our society. Between 2009 and 2010 there were over a million alcohol-related admissions to hospital and figures from 2007 suggested that 10% of men and 4% of women were showing some signs of alcohol dependence. Drug dependency figures are also on the increase, not to mention the increasing numbers of us reporting having fallen prey to modern addictions like obsessive use of internet pornography and social networking sites.

Finding yourself so out of control – however you may rationalise it to yourself – is a miserable experience. Fortunately, whatever form your personal compulsions may take, the evidence is that CBT offers one of the most effective approaches to understanding and managing such difficulties, even if you have reached the point at which your habits or addictions very definitely feel more like cables than cobwebs.

Source: www.CartoonStock.com

Understanding the ties that bind – what is addictive behaviour?

You may have turned to this chapter looking for help in dealing with a very minor annoying habit or an incredibly common problem like smoking or overeating that affects huge numbers of us. If this is the case (and even if you use recreational drugs and smoke a little more cannabis than you suspect is good for you) being invited to lump yourself together with someone struggling with a full-scale opiate addiction or who meets the diagnostic criteria for alcoholism may seem ludicrous, possibly insulting. But please bear with me. Although there are clearly some significant differences between the major addictions and the more trivial, common or garden habits most of us fall into at one time or other, many of the mechanisms underlying these problems, big or small, are remarkably similar. I will be taking several examples from cases of more significant addictions, because the extreme nature of them helpfully illustrates some of the principles involved. But just remember: there is very little advice pertinent to them that does not also apply to the tackling of the minor stuff that, as you probably already know, can still prove remarkably hard to shift.

What's the payoff?

The cognitive behavioural view of addictions and habits regards them all as forms of learned behaviour, reinforced by the rewards they provide for us. It's important to acknowledge that addictions and habits persist because at some level they work for us. They can be genuinely pleasurable and may successfully (if only temporarily) relieve states of pain, tension, boredom or distress. This is why they become such powerfully conditioned responses. Addictions are dysfunctional coping strategies that help us get our needs met: it's just that the way they meet those needs oftens comes at a heavy price. When we have an addiction or indulge a bad habit we want the immediate results; we turn a blind eye to the long-term consequences. Nicotine, caffeine, alcohol, heroin, procrastination, obsessively playing *Angry Birds* into the small hours every night: whatever form our habit takes, it will almost certainly make us feel good or, stop us feeling bad, for at least a while.

Addictions and habits usually take place within specific contexts and they are developed and are kept going with the aid of characteristic thought patterns. Habits and addictions are actually very similar to each other in terms of their underlying mechanisms, varying only with regard to their degree of severity and the level of disruption they cause to your daily life. Some addictions are purely psychological but, when mood-altering substances like cocaine, nicotine, and alcohol are involved, they may create elements of physical dependency as well: the body gets used to the poisons you are putting in and reacts strongly if they are withdrawn.

 insight

Is there such a thing as an addictive personality?

The jury is still out on this question. It does appear that the way the dopamine receptors are distributed in some people's brains may give them poor impulse control and make them vulnerable to abusing stimulants. However, rather than looking for answers in our genes or a specific personality 'type', we would do better to be aware of the character traits and moods that can put us at risk: if we are particularly anxious, impulsive, sensitive or someone who just craves different kinds of altered states, then we need to be on our guard. Invoking the concept of an 'addictive personality' is generally unhelpful, because it can become an excuse. It creates the impression that if we fit the type, we stand little chance of controlling our behaviour, which of course then may become a self-fulfilling prophecy.

Introducing the cognitive model of addiction

The following model illustrates some of the main features of the cognitive model of addiction. These features explain how addictions and habits are established, and why they then become so hard to break.

Aaron Beck proposed that early experiences and key life events create mindsets that dispose some people towards addictive behaviours. For example, if your father was always in the habit of pouring himself a large whiskey after getting in from work, you might have absorbed the belief that 'regularly drinking alcohol is normal and good way to relax'. On the other hand, if you have had the misfortune to suffer trauma or abuse in childhood, the common knowledge that people sometimes use drugs to numb emotional pain or calm themselves down can be all the encouragement you need to start considering using them yourself. Or perhaps social learning mechanisms mean that you have simply copied the bad habits you observed in others?

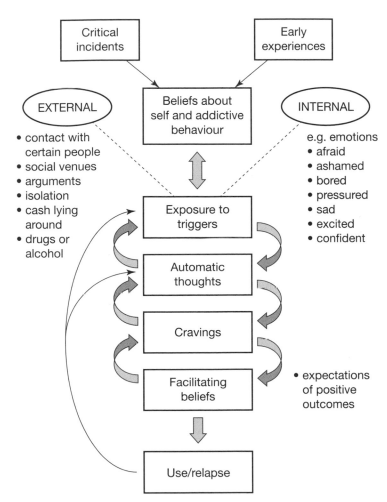

A cognitive behavioural model of addiction

The way we learn to see ourselves can also promote addictive habits. If you are prone to outbursts of rage, or your impulsive behaviour keeps getting you into trouble, you may develop unhelpful core beliefs like, 'I don't have much self-control' or 'My will power is pretty weak'. Put yourself in a setting where someone offers you a cigarette (even though you are trying to give up) and your self-image can end up weakening your resistance to temptation. Repeatedly failed attempts to conquer addictions or overcome habits can also strengthen negative automatic thoughts that such acts of self-control are beyond us.

For most people with addiction issues, exposure to the relevant triggers is usually what brings their good intentions crashing down. These triggers can be *internal* such as unpleasant moods (or euphoric ones for that matter) or *external*, such as the company of particular people or settings that facilitate our habit. These triggers and cues activate your beliefs about whatever it is you are addicted to and cascade negative automatic thoughts that generate powerful cravings: 'Those pub crawls with the lads were just the best'; 'How I'd love to be cashing in a big pile of chips at the end of the evening'; 'Those online girls are just *unbelievably* hot...'; 'I'm going to feel brilliant if I can just get to the next level...'

The human brain is a pattern-making device. It creates connections between things that occur together. Because we learn to associate addictive behaviours and their payoffs with the settings, actions, moods and people that accompany them, just being around those things lowers our resistance and makes us much more likely to fall back into addictive patterns. The smell of cigarette smoke makes us want one, the bright lights, euphoria and pumping rhythms of the club music turn our thoughts to the ecstasy tab we are used to having as part of that experience. This is why lifestyle changes that reduce exposure and access to these triggers are such a crucial aspect of conquering more serious and destructive negative habits.

A key component of the cognitive model is that cravings also prime any number of *facilitating beliefs*. These are the things addicts tell themselves that make it more likely they will yield to temptation. They might include:

- **positive expectations** of the outcome of using or indulging, usually maintained by screening out or dismissing any potential negative consequences (e.g. 'If I take one of these I will be the life and soul of the party ...'; 'One hit and all my troubles will be gone for a while ...')

- **rationalisations** of the addictive behaviour or habit ('A second slice of that cake will taste amazing and will keep me full until lunch time so I won't have to keep on snacking ...')

- **permissive beliefs**: thoughts and attitudes that justify using or indulging ('It's been a tough day: I deserve to relax...'; 'Life's too short not to have fun!')

- **self-efficacy beliefs** that encourage you to see yourself as incapable of resisting ('I have a physical dependency that *makes* me keep using...'; 'I am just a weak person who can't say "no"...').

These beliefs lower resistance to the cravings yet further and commonly precede a lapse. As you can see from the model, this then serves to strengthen the original learned behaviour, reinforces the associated automatic thoughts and beliefs, and makes people more responsive than ever to the relevant cues and triggers in future. 'Bad habits,' someone once said, 'are like a comfortable bed ... easy to get into but hard to get out of ...'. Any behaviour that we repeat often enough becomes a learned response that is ever more likely to just keep replicating itself in the future.

> any behaviour that we repeat often enough becomes a learned response that is ever more likely to just keep replicating itself in the future

In for a penny...

It's not just habit that drives this pattern, it's also what we tell ourselves afterwards. The old saying 'in for a penny, in for a pound' reflects the ethos of what psychologists have called the *abstinence violation effect*. In a nutshell, this means that once we feel we have slipped up, we tend to resign ourselves to further transgressions without putting up much of a fight. We have effectively 'proved' to ourselves that we can't avoid our habit or keep ourselves clean, so we revise our beliefs about our self-efficacy. Seeing ourselves as helpless then increases our chances of acting in a helpless way in future. Also, because we have 'blown it' and the difficulty of resisting is no longer offset by the potential gains of abstinence, part of us feels that we might as well enjoy the pay-off of the addictive behaviour. One slip then becomes the prelude to a massive binge.

Who are you kidding?

Have you ever found yourself ending up in trouble even though you thought you were doing your best to avoid it? This often happens to people with addictions too. While investigating the processes leading to relapse, psychologists Marlatt and Gordon found that addicts made a lot of 'seemingly irrelevant decisions' (SIDs). These amount to self-sabotaging choices that expose people to triggers and cues that can erode their conscious good intentions.

For example, Bill who is trying to give up smoking, ends up mysteriously taking a seat right near the smokers' lounge in the airport, even though there are many others available to him. Jane leaves four bumper bags of crisps in the cupboard because now she's on a diet she knows she will only eat them in moderation. Now sober for two months, Robert decides to take the bus rather than drive to Tara's twenty-fifth birthday bash, even though he knows that previously the knowledge that he is going to have to drive home at the end of the evening has stopped him from drinking. After all, he's not going to be drinking anyway, is he? These innocent, apparently inconsequential choices are not really innocent at all. They are an indirect means of placing yourself in temptation's way, based on an unconscious recognition that when you do so, you are much more likely to fold.

Getting ready to change

Established habits are not easy to break: if they were, addiction wouldn't be such a big social problem and new year's resolutions might have some teeth. Deciding to free yourself from a habit or compulsion is a significant step, and it requires a bit of preparation and planning if it is to stand any realistic chance of working. Often attempts to break habits and addictions fail because people haven't thought through what is likely to be involved, they haven't properly understood the nature of their problem, or because they are not quite ready to change in the first place.

> deciding to free yourself from a habit or compulsion is a significant step

Psychologists James Prochaska and Carlo Di Clemente believe that effective change is not just a one-off decision but the result of a whole process, and one which may have to be repeated several times. In their model, throughout the various 'stages of change' the individual's attitudes, priorities and thought processes evolve. They position themselves towards the prospect of change in new ways, and each stage of change brings with it different tasks and fresh priorities.

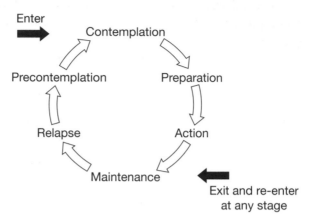

Prochaska and Di Clemente's stages of change model.

Stage one: precontemplation

During the *pre-contemplation stage*, most people are not really prepared to admit to themselves they might have a problem. You may have a sense that something isn't right, but are certainly not quite ready to do anything about it. At this point you will rely on a whole raft of strategies including denial, self-justification and cognitive biases to avoid the issue. So what if you still smoke 50 a day? A few decades ago everyone smoked ... Some people might say that spending four hours in the gym everyday was too much but we all know exercise is good for you and anyway the pounds are just dropping off ... The best thing you can do for yourself at this point is to become more aware of the distortions in your thinking and stop shutting off the negative consequences of your actions.

Stage two: contemplation

If the negative impact of the problem increases, this might move you into the contemplation stage. This is the stage at which you allow yourself to think about the problem or addictive behaviour in a more objective manner in order to reach a decision about the best way to proceed. You will be looking carefully at the pros and cons of the behaviour, considering the benefits and costs of the alternatives, and evaluating what resources you have at your disposal to make a lasting change. A number of techniques and strategies may be useful to you at this point:

1 Keeping a diary in which you look at the frequency of the behaviour, its impact on your life and how it makes you feel throughout the day. There are a number of handy applications now available like *Moodscope* and *Moodjournal* that allow you to do this very easily (see Appendix 2).

2 Performing a costs–benefit analysis that takes into account both the short- and long-term outcomes of the behaviour you are thinking about modifying. The table overleaf is an example of what this might look like. You need to be clear about your motivations. It's going to be tough at times, so you need to convince yourself that change really is worthwhile.

3 Making an inventory of the resources, qualities and experiences that indicate that you may be able to make the change you are thinking about. This might include recalling previous occasions when you have accomplished something difficult, looking at the conditions under which the habit or behaviour seemed to have less of a hold over you and thinking about the people and organisations that might be able to offer you support in your attempts to break the cycle.

4 Collecting the information you need to start creating your personal formulation. This is a vital step as it will form the basis for your action plan, coming up next. Look back at the model of addiction on page 221 and start personalising it. You should be trying to identify the situations in which you are most vulnerable and the internal/external triggers that lower your resistance. You need to isolate any thoughts that make abstinence harder, and those that are likely to make things worse if you do slip up.

An example of a cost–benefit analysis grid

Target behaviour: spending all my free time on internet porn sites

	Positive consequences (gains)	Negative consequences (losses)
Short-term	Exciting Pleasurable Allows me to 'switch off' from real life Feeds and develops my fantasy life	Takes up more and more of my time Stops me from doing other things (spending time with friends/ playing sport) Less and less rewarding the more I do Makes me tired I feel guilty afterwards I find myself looking at more hard-core stuff that I don't feel comfortable with Makes me feel cheap, like I'm getting off at the expense of other people Expensive – big credit card bills
Long-term	Helps me think of myself as a red-blooded guy – someone who isn't prudish about sex	Supports an industry that exploits people Will damage my relationship with Sam Makes me feel ashamed of myself May damage my chances of job promotion if it starts taking over any more of my time.

Stage three: action

This is the point at which your newfound resolution has to be translated into a practical and realistic plan that you stick to. There are a number of principles you should adhere to if you want to create effective change.

Set realistic goals

You must decide what the right targets are for you. For some people, aiming for total abstinence is the way to go since anything less exposes them to cues that increase their risk of relapse. For others, it makes sense to set more modest goals, particularly if you are in the process of tackling a physical dependency: going 'cold turkey' can be so assaulting to your body that many people quickly collapse under the pressure. Sometimes focusing on reducing the quantity of a substance used, or the frequency or duration of critical behaviours creates more sustainable goals that will produce better results in the long term. Crash dieting invariably ends up in subsequent binge eating and the pounds pile back on so you need to think carefully about what you can manage.

> you need to think carefully about what you can manage

Draw up your plan of campaign

On the basis of your formulation you need to determine three things: firstly which negative or unhelpful thoughts or beliefs you are going to change and how to go about it, secondly how you are going to reduce your exposure to cues and triggers, and finally how you are going to deal with cravings and urges when they do arise.

Attack the thoughts that support your habit

From a cognitive behavioural perspective, working with the thoughts that drive addictive behaviour is no different from tackling other thoughts that are unhelpful. It is still a question of identifying the biases, distortions and unwarranted assumptions, and then mobilising evidence to help us replace our negative thinking with more balanced and productive alternatives. Try to notice which thoughts are the most toxic for you and target those if you can.

> working with the thoughts that drive addictive behaviour is no different from tackling other thoughts that are unhelpful

Use the techniques described in Chapter 4 to interrogate and revise your negative assumptions, as Francine has started to do below in a thought record that relates to her compulsive shopping habit.

Automatic thoughts	Case for	Case against	More balanced/ alternative thought
There's nothing I can do to control my shopping habit ...	Over the past two weeks I have spent over £500 on shoes I cannot afford.	In the six months before I was doing really well. I'd actually paid off three of my credit cards. The only luxury items I bought in July were birthday presents.	It's sometimes difficult for me to resist the urge to spend money on myself but past experience suggests I can cut back when I put my mind to it.

Automatic thoughts	Case for	Case against	More balanced/ alternative thought
If I don't cheer myself up with expensive little treats I will get really low.	I do get low moods and sometimes buying things for myself online makes me feel more special for a while and I look forward to them coming.	The happiest time of my life was when I was working on the kibbutz and I wasn't spending anything then! The stress from all the money I owe makes me really fed up and unhappy at times.	The relief I get from buying things doesn't last and it has a more negative impact on my mood longer term. I need to keep practising other ways to manage my feelings that work much better.

When tackling the thought patterns that drive addictive and habit-forming behaviour, it's also a good idea to observe the following four principles:

1 Target the right beliefs

As with all CBT interventions, it's important to be wise about selecting the beliefs that you are going to target. As you have constructed your formulation you will probably have become aware of certain beliefs that play a particularly important part in keeping the addiction or habit going, while others play more supporting roles. If you can effectively modify these key cognitions then it makes it much easier to bring the edifice of your addiction crashing down, although you can also start by chipping away at less central beliefs until the plausibility of the whole structure is weakened. For example, in the case of Paul, who has a gambling addiction, a critical belief might be, 'If I can just win big one time, then it will make up for

> targeting the right beliefs successfully can significantly reduce the hold of your addiction

all the money I've lost over the years ...' whereas examples of less key (but still significant) cognitions might be: 'I like the excitement that comes with knowing I might have a winning ticket in my pocket' and 'Being part of the Friday night poker game takes my mind off work and allows me to relax with my friends ...' It is probably a good idea to target at least one or two critical beliefs relatively early on because otherwise your resolution to get on top of your problem may wane over time.

2 Get specific

In tackling habits and addictions it is particularly important to make your negative automatic thoughts as concrete and specific as you can. Thoughts relating to addictive behaviours can be notoriously and even deliberately vague, which makes them hard to get a purchase on or counteract effectively.

For example, the belief 'Drugs make my life bearable' is hard to grapple with because it is so general. To get to the underlying NATs use techniques like the downward arrow technique (page 66) or interrogate the belief using relevant lines of questioning:

- In what ways do I think my life would be unbearable if I didn't use drugs?
- In what ways do I believe my use of drugs helps me?
- What did I experience and do during those periods when I used drugs less than at present?
- What problems are drugs solving for me and how are they doing that?

3 Get your facts right

Ignorance may not be bliss but it certainly helps if you intend to keep on abusing drugs, alcohol or nicotine. In order to justify our addictions we often need to keep ourselves in a state of semi-ignorance about the reality of the consequences of our habits. We may even deliberately

ignorance may not be bliss but it certainly helps if you intend to keep on abusing cultivate misconceptions that make us feel more comfortable about continuing as we are. For example, people who use drugs or rely on alcohol often deny the health risks involved or entertain false beliefs about the substances they use and how damaging they are.

If you are serious about overcoming your addiction you may need to equip yourself with accurate information about your habit. There are many unbiased and reliable sources of information available online (such as www.talktofrank.com for substance abusers). The facts you find on such sites can be invaluable in arming you to challenge false beliefs about your addiction.

4 Use experiments to test your addiction beliefs

Most addictions and habits take the form of behaviours, so the related thoughts often lend themselves to behavioural experiments that can be a powerful means of refuting them. The following are a few examples of the addiction-related beliefs that might be amenable to experimental investigation:

- *Beliefs about the perceived negative impact of reducing the habit/addiction.* For example, Cal decides to explore her belief that 'stimulants make me work better' by comparing her productivity during a month in which she drinks her habitual eight cups of double-shot espresso and one in which she limits herself to two a day.

- *Beliefs about your inability to cope with your moods without the help of drugs, food or alcohol.* For example, Nadine decides to test her conviction that 'filling myself up with food is the only way I can manage to handle the pain that my loneliness causes me' by sampling and rating her mood every 10 minutes for an hour after her customary binging cycle and then rating her mood if she spends the hour reading through a pile of magazines instead of overeating.

- *Beliefs about the importance of limiting exposure to triggers.* For example, Darryl decides to keep a cravings diary to monitor the amount of cannabis he smokes over a period when he spends time with fellow 'dope-head' Nick and a period when he avoids Nick's company to test out his belief that 'being with Nick doesn't necessarily mean I will smoke more weed'.

● *Beliefs about the rewards and performance benefits of addictive behaviour.* For example, Geoff decides to examine his belief that 'when I've had a drink beforehand, I am less tongue-tied and other people relate to me better' by asking his friend Jamal to observe any difference in the reactions of party guests to him if he presents sober, compared with the reactions he gets at the next event when he arrives with a good few pints inside him.

Implement behavioural changes that weaken your habit

The main thrust of your work in this area is firstly to reduce your exposure to both internal and external cues that keep your habit or addiction going and secondly to put in place lifestyle changes that will help you feel better about yourself and support a habit-free existence.

Obviously if you have a physical dependency on a class A drug or a serous alcohol addiction, one of the first steps may be to undergo a process of physical de-toxification. If you fall into this category you are strongly recommended to seek professional help because some detox regimes are best conducted in in-patient settings, where you can also be given appropriate follow-up and support. Please don't let embarrassment or any other factor prevent you from consulting your GP if you fall into this category and think you might benefit from this kind of help.

Develop new skills

Your action plan should incorporate the development of any new skills you might need to learn or that will reinforce healthier beliefs. For example, you might decide to take a yoga class to help you relax, so you have resources to help you cope with any stressful feelings.

 **tip**

If your addiction is connected with your body in some way, doing regular exercise or even booking some sessions with a personal trainer at the gym can give you something else to focus on, get you out of the house on a regular basis and increase your sense of self-efficacy as you watch yourself achieving your fitness goals. For people who use substances of various kinds, doing something physical and actually taking care of their bodies can underline a really helpful message that their priorities have changed. Exercise also releases natural endorphins that make you feel much better and can counteract any physical effects of withdrawal.

Take practical steps to prepare for temptation

Planning what you can do physically when cravings take hold is also a helpful precaution. Perhaps you could identify a favourite walk you will take yourself on or make sure you get in a ready supply of DVDs to give you something else to focus on when the cravings get bad.

Keep yourself out of harm's way

The most crucial aspect of behavioural change when tackling addictions is being very clear with yourself abut the behaviours and settings that make it harder for you to resist and developing a routine that keeps you well away from these fatal triggers. In the action phase you may have to take alternative routes getting from A to B in order to stay out of harm's way. If your route to work happens to take you past your dealer's house you are likely to end up in trouble. Find an alternative route.

Be careful of the company you keep

If you are serious about getting on top of an addiction, you must identify and stay away from people who encourage your habit.

It's hard to give up smoking if you hang out with smokers, or drinking if you allow yourself to spend every evening in the pub. The chances are today's orange juice will become tomorrow's rum and coke.

Extinguish opportunities for relapse

This is also where activity scheduling comes in. If you know from your diary that you are most vulnerable to your habit in the two hours when you come in from work before your evening meal, then fix up a regular meeting with a friend or take a class during that window to make sure you don't end up on your own with time on your hands and opportunity to succumb.

Schedule in alternatives

However, it's much easier to hold out if you have given yourself something else to do instead. Most serious addictions consume huge amount of people's time and resources. Perhaps you can motivate yourself by investing some of the time and money you get back into doing something you've always wanted to achieve for yourself, or in finding alternative ways to enjoy yourself? However, unless you schedule it in, it may very well never happen.

 **brilliant** tip

Habit-proof your environment

Rid your home of as many cues and triggers as you can. If looking in mirrors activates negative thoughts about how ugly and fat you look, then take them down and use a pocket mirror when you really need to. Don't be tempted to test your willpower by leaving addiction or habit-related paraphernalia around the house. Perhaps you know that having loose cash at home is fatal for you because when you see it you thoughts turn immediately to spending it on drugs? Whenever possible try to addiction-proof your environment so it feels safe for you.

Dealing with cravings and urges

If you are considering changing any established pattern of behaviour it is very important not to be naïve. You are going to be tempted to slip back into your old ways, and remember, the habit established itself in the first place because you find it so seductive. You mustn't underestimate this. Be aware, especially in the early stages before alternative healthier habits have had a chance to take root, that you will inevitably be confronted with cravings.

> the habit established itself in the first place because you find it so seductive

Research suggests that people who plan ahead and who have decided *beforehand* what they will do when temptation strikes stand a much better chance of getting through their cravings.

However, the trick is to stay firm when your cravings are screaming at you. The following techniques may be of assistance.

Get out of there NOW!

Addictive behaviour occurs in particular contexts. Make a deal with yourself that if you find yourself weakening you will stop what you are doing and quickly remove yourself from the situation in which the craving has become acute. That might mean going for an impromptu walk or taking yourself to a public place where you won't have the opportunity to pursue your habit. It might mean excusing yourself from a social gathering in which drugs or alcohol have started triggering unwanted thoughts.

Surf the urge

Like anxiety, cravings have a natural life cycle. They build to a peak and then, if you don't gratify them, after a while they really will subside and leave you alone. The trick is to stay the course. Just acknowledging the wave-like trajectory of a craving, and learning how long they take to die down, can be really helpful. The mindfulness approach emphasises that if we do battle with our feelings they are likely to gain greater control, whereas if we step back, notice and accept them for what they are – just feelings that we don't necessarily have to act upon – we can allow them to pass out of our minds much more easily.

Distract yourself

When you find yourself preoccupied with thoughts about your habit or addiction, try to fill your mind with something else. This might involve giving yourself a task that will absorb your resources like doing a puzzle or a crossword, or applying yourself to a hobby or pastime that you find interesting or enjoyable. It might mean taking a bath or going for a run – doing something that will generate alternative sensations in your body. Perhaps you need to phone a friend or direct your attention towards someone else.

Refocus your motivation

Remind yourself of the gains in both the short- and long-term quadrants of your costs–benefits analysis grid. Also mentally re-run the costs of not getting on top of your addiction. Cravings have a habit of shutting down our access to the future; they are all about immediate gratification in the here and now. Under their influence your head will be full of images of how great it would be if you allowed yourself a cigarette, a drink, a line of cocaine, a tub of ice cream. At this point you need to 'unfreeze' time and play the movie forward into the future when you have to pick up the pieces and deal with the consequences of your lapse.

brilliant tip

In case of emergency break glass!

Some people deliberately create an image of their very worst-case scenario – the lowest point to which their addiction could lead them – and then lock it away in a little red box in their head so that if they feel their resistance is about to collapse they can get it out, contemplate the full horror of it, and generate fresh resolve.

Employ positive self-talk

In 1972 psychologist Walter Mischel conducted a famous investigation into willpower with four to six year olds. He offered them the opportunity to eat one marshmallow straight away or, if they could just wait until the experimenter came back in the room, they could have two. The children who managed to hold out were more often than not those who talked themselves through the situation, reminding themselves of the reward that lay ahead and encouraging themselves to be strong. When faced with temptation it's useful to keep telling yourself why you need to resist, and to rehearse positive self-statements that encourage you to believe that you can!

Use flashcards

Sometimes it's hard to use or even remember the techniques described above. Some people find it really helpful to have a pack of cards with them which summarises really succinctly how they should respond and what they should be doing when temptation strikes. Restrict your messages to very brief instructions and exhortations.

exercise   Create your own top ten

Imagine you are facing a craving right now. Write out a list of five positive self-statements that you think might help you stay strong in the face of temptation and commit them to memory. Now prepare a set of five flash cards, each containing one brief phrase that summarises what a good friend or counsellor would advise you to do in that situation.

Stage four: maintenance

Things are going well. You've followed the plan, done all the things you should and it seems to be working. You can feel your habit, addiction or compulsion starting to loosen its grip on you. You're feeling good about yourself, more positive about life. This is surely the time you can relax and congratulate yourself for a job well done ... Well, actually no. This is ironically precisely the time when you are most vulnerable to relapse, at the very point when you feel you have turned the corner. The problem is that people in the maintenance phase often get complacent.

 **insight**

People doing well in recovery get lulled into a sense of false security. It is for this very reason that organisations like Alcoholics Anonymous don't like their members to talk about being 'cured' and urge them to keep attending meetings at which speakers, however long sober, always introduce themselves with the phrase, 'Hello my name is Martin and I'm an alcoholic ...' This is not to humiliate them but to keep them on their guard. Organisations like AA know how easy it is to relapse, even if you appear to be well in control of your habit or addiction.

It's important and right to celebrate your victories and the passing of significant milestones in your fight against addiction or the habits that have dogged you. We all need encouragement and such markers remind us that we can be strong. However, we also need to keep monitoring our progress, keep ourselves away from triggers, and use the respite from cravings to build up our resilience. This might be the opportunity, for example, to see a therapist about the childhood abuse that primed your gambling habit in the first place. You also need to keep an eye on yourself, checking you aren't making any of those risk-laden 'seemingly irrelevant decisions' or sneakily replacing one addiction with another.

Stage five: relapse

Not a cheery note to end on, I appreciate, but the point is that Prochaska and Di Clemente's cyclical model is a cycle. You may re-enter it at different points but the reality is that most of us will go round it more than once. Relapse, while not inevitable, is very normal. The thing that does the damage is usually not so much the relapse itself, but what happens to people in the wake of it. We have already mentioned the 'abstinence violation effect', when people relinquish control completely after a slip. It is after you have found yourself giving in to your habit or addictive behaviour that you most need to gather your resources and determination to regroup, reset and resist the urge to throw the baby out with the bathwater.

Tell yourself that relapse is a normal part of recovery (because it is). Think of it like a military campaign. Losing one battle doesn't normally mean losing the war; it's the repeated loss of battles that causes you grief. If you fall off the wagon, simply pick yourself up and dust yourself down. Remind yourself it's a long game and use thought records to challenge all the negative and unhelpful thoughts that will inevitably be crowding into your head. Revisit your goals and adjust them if necessary. Review your original motivation and remind yourself why it's worth persisting. Think about the point at which it makes most sense to re-enter the Stages of Change wheel. If you do this properly there are many people out there who can testify to the fact that, however many times you relapse on the way there, you can still ultimately be victorious and get to the point where you control your addictions and habits rather than the other way round.

However, if you are battling significant addiction problems, please don't try to go it alone. Whatever the nature of your addiction or compulsive habit, there are many dedicated groups and organisations out there very used to offering guidance to people struggling with the same issues you are facing. Cognitive behavioural techniques can be powerful, and many drug and alcohol services use them, but they are much more likely to work for you if you have some proper, experienced support behind you while you attempt to apply them.

> if you are battling significant addiction problems, please don't try to go it alone

Afterword: over to you now

Having read this book, I trust you now have a better sense of what cognitive behavioural therapy is all about and how it might help you. CBT is by no means the only type of therapy out there, and it might not even be the best one for you. However, as a useful way of conceptualising many of the difficulties that we may face and offering a range of practical tools for addressing them, potentially it has a lot to offer most of us.

I hope you have found this book helpful and the instructions clear, but if you do find yourself struggling to get the techniques and strategies described here to work for you, please don't give up. It takes time to learn new skills and self-discipline to keep going with them. I have included some tips in Appendix 4 to help you iron out potential teething troubles but, if all else fails, do seek help from a qualified practitioner.

And now it simply remains for me to wish you the very best of luck. With a little application and a following wind you should soon be swatting your NATs with relative ease but remember: CBT isn't a magic bullet. Don't be surprised if it feels like hard work to start with. After all, you are attempting to unlearn habits, thoughts and assumptions that you have probably been rehearsing and consolidating for a very long time. However, keep going and follow the advice carefully, and there is a good chance that you will see results. The comedian 'Professor'

Irwin Corey once remarked that, 'If we don't change direction soon, we will end up where we're going.' So if you're not too happy with some aspect of your current destination, perhaps it is time for an overhaul of your thought life? If you feel it is, I will be delighted if this book plays some small role in helping you reorient yourself towards a better, more enjoyable future.

brilliant recap

We've covered a lot of ground in this book but there are a few key points that I hope you will take with you:

- Our thoughts, feelings and actions all influence each other. Being aware of how they interact can help us create effective strategies for change.

- We need to be aware that we seldom see things objectively. Be on the look out for characteristic thinking traps that can distort your vision of the world and help create unwanted moods and behaviours.

- When dealing with automatic thoughts, always ask yourself: 'What's the evidence for this belief?' Consider alternatives that are more helpful, more accurate or more logical.

- Put your beliefs to the test with behavioural experiments, but design them well so that they answer specific questions or allow you to make meaningful comparisons.

- Appreciate that reprogramming established patterns of thinking can be a long hard slog, but it is possible and the results are usually worth it.

References and further reading

General

Beck, J. (1995) *Cognitive Therapy: Basics and Beyond*. Guilford Press.

Bennett-Levy, J., Butler, G., Fennell, M., Hackmann, A., Mueller, M. and Westbrook, D. (2004) *Oxford Guide to Behavioural Experiments in Cognitive Therapy*. Oxford University Press.

Crane, R. (2008) *Mindfulness-Based Cognitive Therapy: Distinctive Features*. Routledge.

Edelman, S. (2006) *Change Your Thinking*. ABC Books.

Flaxman, P. E., Blackledge J. T. and Bond, F. W. (2010) *Acceptance and Commitment Therapy: Distinctive Features*. Routledge.

Fonagy, A., Roth, P., Parry, G., Target, M. and Woods, R. (eds) (2006) *What Works for Whom? A Critical Review of Psychotherapy Research*. Guilford Press.

Greenberger, D. and Padesky, C. A. (1995) *Mind Over Mood: Change how you feel by changing the way you think*. Guilford Press.

Hawton, K., Salkovskis, P. M. and Clark, D. M. (eds) (1989) *Cognitive Behaviour Therapy for Psychiatric problems – A practical guide*. Oxford University Press.

Hayes, S. C. (2011) *Acceptance and Commitment Therapy: The Process and Practice of Mindful Change*. Guilford Press.

Kabat-Zinn, J. (1990) *Full Catastrophe Living*. Delacorte Press.

McKay, M., Wood, J. C. and Brantley, J. (2007) *The Dialectical Behavior Therapy Skills Workbook: Practical DBT Exercises for Learning Mindfulness, Interpersonal Effectiveness, Emotion Regulation, and Distress Tolerance*. Self-Help Workbook. New Harbinger.

McMulin, R. E. (2000) *The New Handbook of Cognitive Therapy Techniques*. Norton.

Ryle, A. and Kerr, I. B. (2002) *Introducing Cognitive Analytic Therapy: Principles and Practice*. Wiley-Blackwell.

Salkovskis, P. (1997) *Frontiers of Cognitive Therapy: The State of the Art and Beyond*. Guilford Publications.

Seligman, M. (1991) *Learned Optimism*. A. A. Knopf.

Seligman, M. (2003) *Authentic Happiness*. Nicholas Brealey.

Westbrook, D., Kennerley, H. and Kirk, J. (2007) *An Introduction to Cognitive Behaviour Therapy: Skills and Applications*. Sage.

Young, J. E., Klosko, J. S. and Weishaar, M. E. (2003) *Schema Therapy: A Practitioner's Guide*. Guilford Press

Depression

Basco, M. R. (2006) *The Bipolar Workbook*. Guilford Press.

Beck, A. T., Rush, A. J., Shaw, B. F. and Emery, G. (1979) *Cognitive Therapy of Depression*. Guilford Press.

Goodwin, F. K. and Jamison, K. R. (2007) *Manic Depressive Illness*. Oxford University Press.

Miklowitz, D. (2002) *The Bipolar Disorder Survival Guide*. Guilford Press.

Williams, C. (2006) *Overcoming Depression*. Hodder Arnold.

Williams, M., Teasdale, J., Segal, Z. and Kabat-Zinn, J. (2007) *The Mindful Way Through Depression: Freeing Yourself from Chronic Unhappiness*. Guilford Press.

Anger

Davies, W. (2008) *Overcoming Anger and Irritability*. Basic Books.

Freeman, D., Freeman, J. and Garety, P. (2006) *Overcoming Paranoid and Suspicious Thoughts*. Robinson.

Potter-Efron, R. and Potter-Efron, P. (1995) *Letting Go of Anger: The 10 Most Common Anger Styles and What to do About Them*. New Harbinger Publications.

Semmelroth, C. and Smith, D. (2004) *The Anger Habit: Proven Principles to Calm the Stormy Mind*. Sourcebooks.

Anxiety

Benson, H. (1998) *The Relaxation Response*. Avon.

Bourne, E. J. (2005) *The Anxiety & Phobia Workbook*. New Harbinger Publications.

Butler, G. (2009) *Overcoming Social Anxiety & Shyness*. Robinson.

Clark, D. A. (2006) *Cognitive-behavioral Therapy for OCD*. Guilford Press.

Edelman, S. (2006) *Change Your Thinking with CBT: Overcome Stress, Combat Anxiety and Improve Your Life*. Vermilion.

Freeston, M. and Meares, K. (2008) *Overcoming Worry*. Robinson.

Herbert, C. and Wetmore, A. (1999) *Overcoming Traumatic Stress: A Self-help Guide Using Cognitive Behavioural Techniques*. Robinson.

Hyman, B. M. and Pedrick, C. (1999) *The OCD Workbook – Your Guide to Breaking Free from Obsessive Compulsive Disorder.* New Harbinger Publications.

Kennerley, H. (1997) *Overcoming Anxiety: A Self-help Guide Using Cognitive Behavioural Techniques.* Robinson.

Wells, A. (1997) *Cognitive Therapy of Anxiety Disorders: A practice manual and conceptual guide.* Wiley.

Williams, C. (2003) *Overcoming Anxiety: A Five Areas Approach.* Hodder Arnold.

Woolfolk, R. L. and Richardson, F. C. (1978) *Stress, Sanity and Survival.* Signet.

Social phobia

Antony, M. and Swinson, R. P. (2008) *Shyness and Social Anxiety Workbook: Proven, Step-by-step Techniques for Overcoming Your Fear.* New Harbinger Publications.

Butler, G. (1999) *Overcoming Social Anxiety and Shyness: A Self-help Guide Using Cognitive Behavioural Techniques.* Robinson.

Hope, D., Heinberg, R. G., Juster, H. A. and Turk, C. L. (2000) *Managing Social Anxiety: Client Workbook: A Cognitive Behavioural Therapy Approach.* Oxford University Press.

Self-esteem

Fennell, M. (2009) *Overcoming Low Self-Esteem: A Self-help Guide using Cognitive Behavioral Techniques.* Robinson.

Gilbert, P. (2010) *The Compassionate Mind.* Constable.

Lindenfield, G. (2001) *Assert Yourself: Simple Steps to Getting What You Want.* Thorsons.

McKay, M. and Fanning, P. (2000) *Self Esteem: A proven program of cognitive techniques for assessing, improving and maintaining your self-esteem (third edition).* New Harbinger Publications.

Addiction and self-control

Blaszczynski, A. (2010) *Overcoming Compulsive Gambling*. Robinson.

Claiborn, J. and Pedrick, C. (2003) *The Habit Change Workbook: How to Break Bad Habits and Form Good Ones*. New Harbinger.

Epstein, E. (2009) *Overcoming Alcohol Use Problems: Therapist Guide: A cognitive-behavioural treatment program*. OUP USA.

Perkins, K., Conklin, C. and Levine, M. D. (2007) *Cognitive-Behavioral Therapy for Smoking Cessation: A Practical Guidebook to the Most Effective Treatments*. Practical Clinical Guidebooks. Routledge.

Spada, M. (2006) *Overcoming Problem Drinking*. Robinson.

Miscellaneous conditions

Baucom, D. and Epstein, N. (1990) *Cognitive–behavioral Marital Therapy*. Brunner/Mazel Inc.

Cooper, P. J. (1993) *Bulimia Nervosa and Binge-eating: A Guide to Recovery*. Robinson.

Downing-Orr, K. (2010) *Beating Chronic Fatigue: Your step-by-step guide to complete recovery*. Piatkus.

Fairburn, C. (1995) *Overcoming Binge Eating*. Guilford Press.

Freeman, C. (2009) *Overcoming Anorexia Nervosa*. Robinson.

Kennerley, H. (2000) *Overcoming Childhood Trauma*. Robinson.

Otis, J. (2007) *Managing Chronic Pain: Workbook: A Cognitive-Behavioural Therapy Approach*. Oxford University Press.

Williams, M. (2002) *The PTSD Workbook*. New Harbinger.

Studies referred to in text

Clark, D. M. (2011) 'Implementing NICE guidelines for the psychological treatment of depression and anxiety disorders: The IAPT experience', *International Review of Psychiatry*, 23: 375–84.

Gulliksson M., *et al.* (2011) 'Randomized Controlled Trial of Cognitive Behavioral Therapy vs Standard Treatment to Prevent Recurrent Cardiovascular Events in Patients With Coronary Heart Disease', *Archives of Internal Medicine*, 171(2): 134–40.

Kessler, D., Lewis, G., Kaur, S., Wiles, N., King, M., Weich, S., Sharp, D. J., Araya, R., Hollinghurst, S. and Peters, T. J. (2009) 'Therapist-delivered internet psychotherapy for depression in primary care: a randomised controlled trial', *The Lancet*, (374) 9690: 628–34.

LaFrance, W. C., Miller, I. W., Ryan, C. E., Blum, A. S., Solomon, D. A., Kelley, J. E. and Keitner, G. I. (2009) 'Cognitive behavioral therapy for psychogenic nonepileptic seizures', *Epilepsy Behaviour*, 14(4): 591–96.

Laithwaite, H., Gumley, A., O'Hanlon, M., Collins, P., Doyle, P., Abraham, L., *et al.* (2009). 'Recovery after psychosis (RAP): A compassion focused programme for individuals in high security settings', *Behavioural and Cognitive Psychotherapy*, 37: 511–26.

Mann, E., Smith, M. J., Hellier, J., Balabnovic, J. A., Hamed, H., Grunfield, E. A. and Hunter, M. S. (2012) 'Cognitive behavioural treatment for women who have menopausal symptoms after breast cancer treatment (MENOS 1): a randomised controlled trial', *The Lancet Oncology*, 13(3): 309–18.

Marlatt, G. A. and Gordon, J. R. (1985) *Relapse Prevention: Maintenance Strategies in the Treatment of Addictive Behaviors.* Guilford Press.

Mitcheson, L., Maslin, J., *et al.* (2010) *Applied Cognitive and Behavioural Approaches to the Treatment of Addiction.* John Wiley & Sons.

Nauert, R. (2012) 'Cognitive-Behavioral Therapy helps traumatized kids heal'. Summary of the Queen's University of Belfast press release of 24 May, posted on PsychCentral (http://psychcentral.com/news/2012/05/25/cognitive-behavioral-therapy-helps-traumatized-kids-heal/39234.html).

Prochaska, J. O. and Di Clemente, C. C. (1983) 'Process and stages of self-change of smoking: Towards an integrative model of change', *Journal of Consulting and Clinical Psychology*, (51): 390–95.

Useful websites

www.alcoholics-anonymous.org.uk/

Well-known organisation providing support for problem drinkers.

www.talktofrank.com/

Reliable information about drugs and substance misuse.

www.nhs.uk/Depression

Information about depression and NHS-based treatment options.

www.nimh.nih.gov/health/publications/depression/

American site that provides useful information about depressive disorders.

www.depressionalliance.org

UK charity for people suffering from effects of depression.

www.social-anxiety.org.uk

Charity offering support for social phobia.

www.nimh.nih.gov/health/topics/anxiety-disorders/index.shtml

American site: a good source of information about the various forms of anxiety and discussion of treatment options.

www.nhs.uk/conditions/anger-management

Health Service advice regarding anger management.

www.ocduk.org

Information and support for sufferers of Obsessive Compulsive Disorder and their families.

www.something-fishy.org/

Very informative site about all aspects of eating disorders.

www.bps.org.uk/

The British Psychological Society website. Contains a feature allowing you to locate a qualified clinical psychologist in your area.

www.mind.org.uk/

Well-established mental health charity that can provide up-to-date information and support for a wide variety of mental health issues.

www.babcp.com

Main site for British Association for Behavioural and Cognitive Psychotherapies with a 'Find a Therapist' link.

www.getselfhelp.co.uk

An excellent source of free CBT resources including sheets to download.

Appendix 1

Brilliant directory of online CBT courses, computer-based tools and smartphone applications

Name	Description	Address	Platform	Sharing	Cost
Mood Gym	Excellent interactive online course teaching CBT techniques for depression.	http://moodgym.anu.edu.au/welcome	Web-based	☒	FREE
Living Life to the Full	Series of online presentations on CBT techniques for a number of common problems.	http://www.llttf.com/	Web-based	☒	FREE
Living Life TV	Polished series of 10-minute online video presentations introducing CBT techniques for issues like sleep problems, confidence, problem-solving and assertiveness.	http://www.llttf.tv/	Web-based	☒	FREE

Name	Description	Address	Platform	Sharing	Cost
FearFighter Panic and Phobia treatment	NICE endorsed interactive treatment programme for panic and phobias. Nine steps that take approximately 30 minutes each to complete. Very thorough and thoughtfully designed.	http://www.fearfighter.com/	Web-based	☑	PAID*
Beating the Blues	NICE recommended online intervention for depression and anxiety. Treatment programme of eight 50-minute weekly sessions.	http://www.beatingtheblues.co.uk/	Web-based	☒	PAID*
Good Days Ahead	Online course tackling anxiety and depression.	http://www.empower-interactive.com/	Web-based	☑	PAID
The Wellness Shop	Online interactive training for CBT techniques to deal with anxiety, insomnia and depression.	http://thewellnessshop.co.uk/products	Web-based	☒	PAID
HealthMedia Solutions	An American range of 'digital health coaching' programmes covering topics such as smoking, stress, depression, binge eating, back pain. Uses your information to generate a personalised plan.	http://www.healthmedia.com	Web-based	☒	PAID

Name	Description	Address	Platform	Sharing	Cost
MoodScope	Excellent mood tracking software that can help you improve awareness and identify triggers for low mood. Programme also alerts selected friends or professionals if your mood dips significantly.	http://www.moodscope.com	Web-based	☑	FREE
MoodTracker	Mood tracking software for people with depression or bipolar disorder. Includes a personal history section to help you keep track of your medication and alerts can be set to remind you to take it or to notify friends/professionals if you are experiencing a manic episode.	https://www.moodtracker.com	Web-based + Windows 7 phone app	☑	FREE
MoodPanda	Mood tracking software.	http://moodpanda.com	Web-based + iPhone app	☒	FREE

Name	Description	Address	Platform	Sharing	Cost
Moodjournal	Journal your moods and identify lifestyle triggers. Includes reminder functions and a useful feature allowing you to see how physical activity impacts on your mood.	http://www.moodjournalportal.com	Web-based, iPhone and Android apps	☒	FREE
iThinkSmarter	Individualised interactive self-help CBT guide for a growing number of conditions.	Available on iTunes AppStore	iPhone/iPod/ iPad	☒	PAID
Thought Diary / Thought Diary Pro	Portable app-based version of a thought diary record. No more excuses about not having your diary sheets with you! The more expensive pro version prompts you to identify thinking errors and enter alternative thoughts as well. Very useful.	Available on iTunes AppStore	iPhone/iPod/ iPad	☒	PAID
eCBT	Apps that help you log your NATs and core beliefs, spot thinking errors and challenge them. Currently three apps available for depression, anxiety and trauma. More in development.	Available on iTunes AppStore	iPhone/iPod/ iPad	☒	PAID

Name	Description	Address	Platform	Sharing	Cost
iCBT	App to take you through the thought record process. Allows you to send summary report of key events to your clinician or therapist.	Available on iTunes AppStore	iPhone/ iPod/ iPad	☑	PAID
CBTReferee	Helps you spot thinking errors and generate alternative thoughts by becoming your own 'ref'. Privacy functions.	Available on iTunes AppStore or Google Play store	iPhone/ iPod/ iPad + Android	☒	PAID
Gratitude Journal	Studies show that being grateful can have a positive impact on mood. This app helps remind you to look for positive experiences and log them.	Available on iTunes AppStore	iPhone/ iPod/ iPad	☒	PAID
Live Happy	Cultivate the six 'habits of happiness' identified by leading happiness researcher Sonja Lyubomirsky.	Available on iTunes AppStore	iPhone/ iPod/ iPad	☒	PAID
DBT self help	App to help develop DBT skills of mindfulness, emotion regulation, social competence and distress tolerance.	Available on iTunes AppStore	iPhone/ iPad	☒	PAID

Name	Description	Address	Platform	Sharing	Cost
MoodKit	Very comprehensive app. Journalling of moods and thoughts, challenging of unhelpful cognitions, scheduling of helpful activities, tips and advice.	Available on iTunes AppStore	iPhone/ iPod/ iPad	☒	PAID
Affirmations Inspired by Nature	Nice little app that gives you words of encouragement relevant to the mood you select.	Available on iTunes AppStore	iPhone/ iPod/ iPad	☒	FREE
Cognitive Diary CBT Self-help	Thought logging diary sheet app.	Available on Google Play Store	Android	☒	FREE
Irrational Thinking CBT Test	Helps identify your thinking style and the thought distortions you are prone to.	Available on Google Play Store	Android	☒	FREE
Self-esteem blackboard	App with CBT techniques for improving your self-esteem.	Available on Google Play Store	Android	☒	FREE
PTSD coach	App from the Department of Veteran Affairs to help soldiers identify and use CBT to manage symptoms of PTSD.	Available on Google Play Store	Android	☒	FREE

Name	Description	Address	Platform	Sharing	Cost
Habit Streak	Monitors your progress in cultivating good habits and achieving daily goals. Great for activity scheduling and breaking bad habits/addictions.	Available on Google Play Store	Android	☒	PAID
Habit Factor	Monitors progress in reaching goals and targets.	Available on iTunes AppStore and Google Play Store	iPhone/iPod/iPad + Android	☒	PAID
Sleeping Tips Using CBT	CBT-based app giving sleep hygiene advice.	Available on iTunes	iPhone/iPod/iPad	☒	FREE
Relax melodies	App allows you to select your own combination of soothing sounds to help you relax.	Available on iTunes	iPhone/iPod/iPad	☒	FREE
Simply Being	Guided mindfulness meditation app.	Available on iTunes	iPhone/iPod/iPad	☒	FREE
Deep Relax DM	Guided hypnotherapy for relaxation.	Available on iTunes	iPhone/iPod/iPad	☒	FREE

Appendix 2

Example of a thought record

The situation	Your feelings	Automatic thoughts	Case for ...	Case against ...	Alternative balanced thought	Re-rate moods
Walking back from work at night	Anxious 80% Lonely 20% Scared 70%	Something awful is going to happen to me... I can't cope with feeling like this...	Sometimes people are attacked – and they are more vulnerable if they are on their own. My feelings are telling me that I am in danger.	I have done this trip hundreds of times and nothing bad has happened. I am in a well-lit street and there are lots of people in their houses on either side who I could call on for help if I needed to. When I feel like this I know after a few minutes my panic dies down. I am very close to home now. There is less and less opportunity for anything bad to happen.	I am at some risk but not nearly as high as my feelings are telling me. I have a plan and I could cope with most things that are likely to happen to me.	Anxious 50% Lonely 20% Scared 35%

Appendix 3

Blank forms and thought record templates

Example of thought record

The situation	Your feelings	Automatic thoughts	Case for ...	Case against ...	Alternative balanced thought	Re-rate moods

Activity schedule sheet

	Day:	Day:	Day:	Day:
6.00–8.00 am				
8.00–10.00 am				
10.00–12.00 am				
12.00–2.00 pm				
2.00–4.00 pm				
4.00–6.00 pm				
6.00–8.00 pm				
8.00–10.00 pm				
10.00–12.00 pm				
12.00–2.00 am				
2.00–4.00 am				
4.00–6.00 am				

Exposure worksheet

TARGET FEAR: ....

Date	Form of exposure	Duration of exposure	Anticipated level of difficulty (0–10)	Anxiety level one minute before (0–10)	Highest anxiety during (0–10)	Anxiety level five minutes after (0–10)

A blank incident analysis template

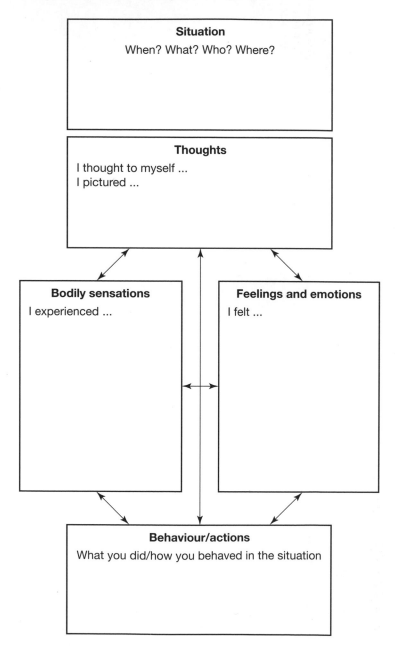

Situation
When? What? Who? Where?

Thoughts
I thought to myself ...
I pictured ...

Bodily sensations
I experienced ...

Feelings and emotions
I felt ...

Behaviour/actions
What you did/how you behaved in the situation

Behavioural experiment sheet

Thought or belief I will test out

Brilliant checklist

☐ Does my experiment actually target my belief?

☐ Are the expected results measurable and/or observable?

☐ Will the results be unambiguous?

☐ Have I operationalised my belief properly?

☐ Does my experiment allow me to make clear predictions?

How I intend to test out my thought or belief

Conviction level before (0–100)	Anticipated results (What I think will happen)	Results (What actually happened)	Learning and new insights	Conviction level of original thought after (0–100)

Appendix 4
What to do if it's not working

A brilliant troubleshooting guide

CBT is a skill and like any new skill you shouldn't be unduly surprised if it feels difficult in the early stages. Sometimes it's not until we start to try to change something that we become aware just how entrenched it has become. If you find yourself struggling then you may find it helpful to ask yourself the following questions.

1 Are you targeting the right beliefs?

Sometimes we can end up trying to work on beliefs that are too vague or general to be helpful to us. Always aim to make your beliefs as specific as you can. You need to get to the level at which the belief has some kind of emotional charge for you. They are called 'hot thoughts' for a reason – they are supposed to make us feel things. If a NAT doesn't have a negative emotional charge then it's probably not the right target. It should make you squirm a bit, or flush with anger, or leave you feeling a bit blue or het up. If your negative thought lacks emotional punch then employ the downward arrow technique on page 66, using the question 'And what would be the worst thing about that?' to press deeper and find the belief that does affect your mood.

2 Are you confident you can make the change?

It's very hard to do anything effectively if a part of you is telling yourself that it's really impossible. Hopefully the examples in this book will give you some confidence in the techniques of CBT but if you are not sure you have set the right goals for yourself, use the ruler below to establish the level to which you believe your current ones are achievable. If the discrepancy between the two scales is too great, you might want to think about changing your goals to ones that are both sufficiently important to keep you motivated but realistic enough for you to have faith in your capacity to reach them.

On a scale of 0–10, 0 being not at all important and 10 being very important, how important is it right now for you to achieve...?

Importance: 0 1 2 3 4 5 6 7 8 9 10

On a scale of 0–10, 0 being not at all confident and 10 being very confident, how confident are you that you would succeed?

Confidence: 0 1 2 3 4 5 6 7 8 9 10

Goal ruler
Adapted from Mitcheson, L. et al (2010)

3 How are you measuring your progress?

We all need to see how we are getting along and reassure ourselves that we are making headway. I was very struck at school by how cross-country runs on familiar routes felt so much shorter and less exhausting than when we attended away competitions in unfamiliar locations. The difference was simply that on home ground I recognised markers along the way that told me how far along the route I was. You need some method to measure your progress. This may be a diary of the intensity or duration of your moods, or a tally of the frequency of key behaviours. It might just be making sure you rate the emotions connected with your negative thoughts so you can see how they change over time as your alternative thoughts become more established. Decide how you will know if your problem is improving and find some way to monitor progress towards your goal.

4 Are you still writing it down?

After a while it is very easy to get blasé about challenging your automatic thoughts and to stop bothering about keeping accurate or sufficiently detailed thought records. Try not to do this, especially in the early stages, because the discipline of writing your thoughts and responses down makes you focus on what you are doing and allows you to evaluate more accurately whether your alternative thoughts are hitting the spot. If they are off beam or don't take all the relevant evidence into account, you are much more likely to spot this if you force yourself to write them out. If you have a smartphone there are several apps that will help you record and rate your negative thoughts and some will even help you identify thinking errors and come up with more balanced alternatives. See Appendix 1 for more details.

5 How much are you mentally rehearsing your new beliefs?

Most of us wouldn't go into an exam having read the textbook only once and be able to rely on being able to answer all the questions. It takes time and repeated exposure for new information to sink in, let alone become second nature. You need to keep repeating your new beliefs to yourself constantly; keep mulling them over and do all you can to reinforce them. Your negative thoughts have run freely in well-worn grooves, but your new alternative thoughts will require a little time and attention if they are to establish themselves as viable rivals.

6 Does your lifestyle support your new beliefs?

It's no good telling yourself one thing in your head if you are subtly giving yourself a very different message with your actions. CBT teaches us that the influence between thoughts, emotions and actions works both ways, so you need to aim for consistency. If you are consciously attempting to install the new belief that 'I am a caring person' but not doing anything to demonstrate that belief either to yourself or the world, it is unlikely to be a very effective antidote to your automatic thoughts about how selfish you are. The messages we get from our behaviour are some of the most powerful and incontrovertible, which is why behavioural experiments can be so useful to us at times. But the downside is that the evidence of our actions can weigh strongly against the voice inside our head if the two don't align.

7 If you are still not making progress, have you considered asking for help?

If you are getting stuck, don't suffer in silence. Go and see a trained CBT practitioner who will be able to help you. For many issues you will be able to see someone for free on the NHS, but there are also many independent private CBT practitioners who will be able to help. Most clinical psychologists will have been trained in CBT and you can also log onto the British Association for Behavioural and Cognitive Psychotherapies (BABCP) website (www.babcp.com) and use its search engine to find a qualified practitioner in your area.

Index